Praise for *The Split*

"Shaun Rein is a consistently challenging thinker and essential guide to anyone trying to make money in complex Chinese markets. *The Split* should be essential reading for any foreign investor trying to understand how a new era of geopolitical upheaval is going to make that task harder still."

James Crabtree, author of *The Billionaire Raj*

"Shaun Rein's *The Split* is a highly readably and richly detailed field guide to foreign business opportunities in China during an era of heightened geopolitical rivalry between the U.S. and accompanying shifts in economic policies and regulation on both sides. Drawing on many years of on-the-ground experience and myriad interviews, Rein offers a nuanced account of which sectors remain promising and which do not and where new challenges may lurk."

Jacques deLisle, Director, Center for the Study of Contemporary China, University of Pennsylvania

T0299700

The Split

The Split

*Finding the Opportunities in China's Economy in
the New World Order*

Shaun Rein

First published by John Murray Business in 2024
An imprint of John Murray Press

5

Copyright © China Market Research Group Ltd 2024

A CIP catalogue record for this title is available from the British Library

Trade Paperback ISBN 978 1 39981 6 397
UK ebook ISBN 978 1 39981 6 410

Typeset by KnowledgeWorks Global Ltd.

Printed and bound in Great Britain by Clays Ltd, Elcograf S.p.A.

John Murray Press policy is to use papers that are natural, renewable and
recyclable products and made from wood grown in sustainable forests.
The logging and manufacturing processes are expected to conform to the
environmental regulations of the country of origin.

John Murray Press
Carmelite House
50 Victoria Embankment
London EC4Y 0DZ

John Murray Business
123 S. Broad St., Ste 2750
Philadelphia, PA 19109

The authorised representative in the EEA is Hachette Ireland,
8 Castlecourt Centre, Dublin 15, D15 XTP3, Ireland (email: info@hbgi.ie)

John Murray Press, part of Hodder & Stoughton Limited
An Hachette UK company

Tom Tom,

To my "Unexpected Innovator": I am so proud of you and your innovations in drones and speakers. Never stop looking at the world differently from everyone else, and following your own path, even if it can be lonely at times. I cannot wait to see you revolutionize mobility, public safety, and the world.

Love,
Baba

Contents

About the Author

Shaun Rein is the founder and managing director of the China Market Research Group (CMR). He works with boards, billionaires, heads of states, CEOs and senior executives of Fortune 500 and leading Chinese companies, private equity firms, SMEs, and hedge funds to develop their China growth and investment strategies.

Rein authored the international bestsellers *The End of Cheap China*, *The End of Copycat China*, and *The War for China's Wallet*. *Publishers Weekly* named *The End of Cheap China* a top-ten business book for 2012. Rein is regularly featured in *The Financial Times*, *The Wall Street Journal*, and *The New York Times*. He regularly appears on CNN, CBS News, and CNBC. Rein is one of the most sought-out keynote speakers focused on innovation, consumer trends, and the economy in China.

Rein graduated from McGill University with a BA Honors in East Asian Studies and from Harvard University with a Master's in Regional Studies: East Asia. He served on the Board of Trustees for St. Paul's School as well as the endowment's investment committee. He has lived in Shanghai, China, since 2003.

Prologue

"After Russia invaded Ukraine, my boss in the US forced us to cancel a multimillion USD software project with a Chinese provincial government," Bill said with a sigh, taking a sip of red wine.

Bill had the presence of a leader. Educated at a leading American business school, he ran the Asia–Pacific region for an American technology firm. His company's technology was years ahead of its Chinese competitors', which was why the provincial government had chosen them over domestic providers, despite the growing split in technology supply chains between China and the US.

Bill had spent months closing the deal and then implementing the project. He was frustrated by the cancellation. Especially disheartening for him was his loss of face with the local government officials with whom he had cooperated for years in his current and previous jobs. Confronted with high KPIs and pressure from officials above, the local officials were upset with Bill because the Americans had backed out of the deal, hurting their potential for promotion.

Bill sighed again as he took another sip of wine. "My boss is worried about getting sanctioned by the US for selling advanced technology to the Chinese government. For him, it was better just to end the project, pay a fine to the client, and stop working with any entities with Chinese government affiliation. He does not want to risk getting sanctioned."

Since I started the China Market Research Group (CMR) in 2005, political risk has always worried my clients. They'd ask: Did I think China's government would allow foreign companies to invest in a regulated sector like the internet, media, or financial services? What about the automotive industry? CEOs asked whether they could manage government relations without running afoul of the US Foreign Corrupt Practices Act. They worried they would have to bribe government officials to get approvals for projects, or hire the son or daughter of a Party member to get deals closed. Many wanted to know how to adhere to censorship regulations without compromising their sense of morality. Executives worried about protectionism, favoring state-owned enterprises (SOEs) in bidding processes for projects. Was it worth submitting bids for projects? Would SOEs only buy domestically?

Until Trump became president, the Chinese government posed the higher political risk. Foreign businesses often ran afoul of Chinese law and were forced to shut down or change business practices. Google closed down the mainland Chinese version of its search engine after refusing to comply with local censorship regulations. Yahoo left China due to data laws, and Facebook never even entered the market, though Chinese clients account for 10 percent of Meta's total 134.9 billion USD revenue.[1] When social media networking site LinkedIn—one of my clients—set up in China, not breaching local content laws was top priority. Eventually, the political risk and data housing laws became too onerous for parent company Microsoft, so it shut LinkedIn down in China.

During the 2010s, the allure of the profit potential outweighed any political risks for most American companies. After all, China had become a major market not just for consumer brands like Porsche, L'Oréal, and KFC, but also for American technology companies like Qualcomm, Nvidia, and

Texas Instruments. From 2013 to 2019, China accounted for over 30 percent of global growth, ranking first in the world according to the IMF.[2] No multinational could afford to ignore China's potential, despite the political risk.

As Chinese firms like Huawei realized more money could be made by innovating than by copying, they became the biggest buyers of advanced technology from American firms like Intel. Collectively, 30 percent of American semiconductor revenues were from sales to China before President Biden limited such sales.[3] Entrepreneurs like Alibaba's Jack Ma became one of the world's richest men by clamping down on counterfeit products sold on his ecommerce sites. Chinese bought more Louis Vuitton handbags than consumers from anywhere in the world, leaving LVMH CEO Bernard Arnault to vie with Elon Musk for title of the world's richest person.

In 2020, China imported 350 billion USD worth of semiconductor chips. In 2022, Qualcomm derived around 67 percent of its 33.5 billion USD in revenues from China, and Intel 43 percent or 21.14 billion USD of its total revenues for the same year.[4] Before US sanctions, Huawei bought 11 billion USD worth of American technology annually.

China as a growth driver for American technology firms ended after President Trump started his trade war over what he called unfair trade imbalances. War hawks in the American Congress like Senators Marsha Blackburn and Tom Cotton and Congressman Mike Gallagher ratcheted up claims that Chinese firms posed a national security threat and pushed to ban sales of technology to China in a move toward decoupling.

Suddenly, the political risk to businesses became more pronounced from the American government than from China. Biden went further than Trump in tightening the vice around Chinese firms. He banned the sale of advanced semiconductors to China and hyped the threat of Chinese new energy vehicles (NEVs) to American national security. He also passed laws requiring all companies sourcing from Xinjiang Province to prove Uyghur slave labor was not used. American border control confiscated hundreds of millions of dollars of sports apparel as well as cars such as Bentleys, as some of their parts were sourced from Xinjiang. Biden's rules essentially mean Chinese, and even American and German, firms are considered guilty until proven innocent of using slave labor if they source from Xinjiang.

Biden dropped the sword of Damocles onto the investment community, banning American venture capitalists from investing in a wide swathe of Chinese technology companies in artificial intelligence and semiconductors to prevent American know-how from reaching China. The result of the sanctions is American technology companies like Bill's have lost profits and their position in the technology supply chain as they are now barred from selling their most innovative technology to Chinese firms. Huawei, for example, had to cut out all American technology firms from the production of its bestselling Mate 60 handset.

Rising fears of political risk under Trump and Biden have made American companies think twice about expanding both manufacturing and sales operations in China. Companies like Foxconn, which makes Apple iPhones, have started to build factories in India and Vietnam where costs are even cheaper than China. Dell announced it would move more of its supply chains to other countries. Dell's China sales plummeted 52 percent year over year after the reported moves as Chinese consumers boycotted them.[5]

Some American firms, like consumer electronics maker GoPro, moved closer to home and started sourcing from Mexico. By 2023, Mexico replaced China as America's largest trading partner, even though many of the factories there are owned by

Chinese. Other companies have tried re-shoring to America but have run into high labor costs and uneven regulation.

Diversifying supply chains, or creating a China Plus One supply chain strategy, is key to minimizing political risk from the American side and in case there is another black swan event like Covid that disrupts shipping lanes. Despite the pressure from the American government to de-risk from China, few American companies have shut their China operations—after all, China still has the best manufacturing ecosystem in the world with best-in-class automation, tax breaks, and infrastructure. China also possesses a labor pool that is more efficient than India's, Vietnam's, and Mexico's.

China remains the key market to sell into as the world's largest retail market as the middle class there continues to grow. China's prime minister Li Qiang announced at the World Economic Forum in Davos in 2024 that he expects China's middle class to swell from 400 million to 800 million over the next decade.[6] Many companies are moving supply chains back to China in order to speed up the go-to-market supply chain to sell into China. Adidas announced it will increase sourcing from China to get products to Chinese consumers more quickly. As one senior executive for adidas told me, "We must source from China for China to speed up our go-to-market time frame."

Despite the political tensions, China should still be the growth driver for American companies in non-politically sensitive sectors. Chinese consumers still clamor to buy foreign brands like Apple, Tesla, and Hoka. They still want to drink Coca-Cola and Budweiser beer and eat American beef and Maine lobsters.

Some analysts argue Vietnam or India is the next China. While I remain optimistic about Vietnam's growth opportunities because of its young and growing middle class, scale matters. If China grows 5 percent annually, that growth alone is like adding an entire Vietnam and Thailand economy. No other country, aside from maybe India, with its 1.4 billion population, has the growth potential that China has. But India's per capita GDP is only one-fifth that of China's. India will not replace China as a growth driver anytime soon.[7]

This book will show executives which sectors still hold promise for foreign companies, like footwear, and which sectors don't anymore, like technology, because of political risk and national security concerns. The days of easy profits are gone as China faces a slowing economy and an aging growth model, but foreign companies that can navigate the economic and consumer shifts will find that China remains a key market for growth.

For Bill's boss, because of risk from America, it was better to cut losses early and look for other opportunities by selling to other Asian markets like Singapore and South Korea that have closer political ties with America. The risk America would ban them from exporting to China was too high to invest in operations to sell to Chinese entities. American technology companies will find that Bill's company is right, and China is no longer a great market to sell into because of political risk from both sides.

Bill's company was simply yet another example for Chinese officials that they can no longer rely on American companies to deliver contracted technology and services. They have concluded that Chinese companies have to build supply chains independent of foreign technology, which is why the government has backed multibillion-dollar private equity funds targeting the semiconductor sector and doled out subsidies to the solar and NEV sectors. Even if they want to buy American technology, Chinese firms worry the US will ban future sales.

The world is splitting between US and China. No government, no company, no person is immune to the rising tension between the world's two superpowers.

Countries must choose if they want to get closer to China's economic orbit or America's. It is virtually impossible to be neutral and trade closely with both. Companies must decide: Do they want to sell into Chinese supply chains or into America's. Most Japanese and South Korean companies have decided to sell into American supply chains and thus have been cut out of the supply chain for Chinese firms. Countries in the Global South, like Saudi Arabia and Kenya, are gravitating closer to China and have doubled down on buying Chinese technology to achieve their own economic ambitions. Everyday consumers cannot hide from The Split. Inflation has become a problem due to a combination of energy shortages and supply chain disruptions triggered by the Russian invasion of Ukraine, loose monetary policy by the US Federal Reserve Bank, and tariffs slapped on Chinese-made goods.

Beijing believes that the US—regardless of who is president—has gone all in to try to contain China's rise. Worries over geopolitics hang over Chinese consumers and businesspeople in the post-Covid era. Instead of investing in new projects or embarking on revenge spending like Americans did after Covid, Chinese businesses and consumers cut back on spending, traded down, and delayed big-ticket purchases like homes. Chinese saw how American sanctions on Cuba, Iran, and North Korea have impoverished generations there and worry the same would happen to China, so they started saving for rainier days.

The Chinese worry that the conflict will last for decades as America tries to waylay the threat to the US-led world order. For its part, China wants more say in international affairs by building up multilateral organizations like BRICS that counter-balance the influence of the G7.

Under Xi, China has also taken a turn back toward socialism to create a more equitable and fairer society. This shift toward socialism makes Chinese and foreign investors alike worry that the antibusiness excesses of Maoism will return. Made uneasy by unclear policymaking, wealthy Chinese are shifting assets outside of China and SME business owners are delaying fixed-asset investment.

Bill's experiences underscore the main theme of this book—the world is splitting between the US and China into a new cold war. Businesses and investors must prepare to navigate The Split. Many pundits argue China is no longer investable and that capital is better deployed in other markets like India or Japan.

It is true that the heyday of quick and easy profitmaking of the early 2000s to mid-2010s is gone, but there remain good opportunities to profit from urbanization, the rise of domestic Chinese technology powerhouses, and the continued growth of China's middle class. Despite the rough waters, there are still ways to profit from China for companies and investors that understand the shifts in consumer trends, policies, and geopolitics. As one chief strategy officer of an iconic German brand told me, "Our growth will come from China and India for the next five years. Those two markets are our growth priority." Similarly, a portfolio manager for one of America's largest mutual funds told me that she remains "bullish and committed to China's long-term growth prospects."

It would be a mistake to bet against the world's second largest economy and to predict its economic collapse, as so many China watchers have predicted over the past 20 years. The IMF predicts China will continue to account for one-third of the world's economic growth for the foreseeable future.[8]

This book seeks to help senior executives and investors understand how the Chinese government is dealing with pressure from America and the structural problems facing its economy, such as an overreliance on the real estate sector and infrastructure for growth. The government has launched initiatives like Common Prosperity and Indigenous Innovation. It has also embarked on charm offensives to the Global South that will create new growth drivers and minimize the impact of lost trade with America. China's old growth playbook relying on real estate for growth is broken—this book will show how the government supports what it has coined New Productive Forces to drive growth, such as advanced manufacturing, renewable energy like solar power and NEVs, and a shift toward services. These new growth drivers bring opportunities for foreign businesses.

Based on over 10,000 interviews with government officials, senior executives, billionaires, and everyday Chinese consumers like factory workers my firm and I have conducted over the past three decades, including the zero-Covid era when I was marooned in China for three years, this book will help businesspeople and investors navigate the changing political winds and profit from China's policy shifts and rising middle class.

Notes

1. Che Pan, "China Accounted for 10 percent of Meta's Sales in 2023 as Chinese Brands Seek Global Exposure," *South China Morning Post*, February 3, 2024, https://www.scmp.com/tech/big-tech/article/ 3250831/china-accounted-10-cent-metas-sales-2023-chinese-brands-seek-global-exposure

2. Eswar S. Prasad, "China Stumbles But is Unlikely to Fall," *International Monetary Fund*, December 2023, https://www.imf.org/en/Publications/fandd/issues/2023/12/China-bumpy-path-Eswar-Prasad

3. Lara Williams, "China to Take Lead in Global Semiconductor Growth," *Investment Monitor*, July 25, 2022, https://www.investmentmonitor.ai/features/china-lead-global-semi-conductor-growth-2030/?cf-view

4. Iain Morris, "After a Two-Year Surge in Sales to China, US Semiconductor Companies Stand to Lose Billion in Revenues as Export Controls are Tightened," *Informa: Light Reading*, March 24, 2023, https://www.lightreading.com/semiconductors/us-chip-exposure-to-china-grew-even-more-last-year#close-modal

5. Zhang Yushuo and Fan Xuehan, "Dell Won't Drop China Factories, SVP Wu Says," *Yicai Global*, November 28, 2023, https://www.yicaiglobal.com/news/20231128-22-dell-will-not-exit-china-factories-svp-says#:~:text=Dell%20had%208%20percent%20of

6. Li Qiang, "Chinese Premier Li Qiang Lays Out Proposals for Rebuilding Global Trust and China's Economic Vision," Speech at World Economic Forum at Davos, January 16, 2024, https://www.weforum.org/press/2024/01/chinese-premier-rebuilding-global-trust/

7. World Bank, "GDP per Capita," *World Bank Data*, https://data.worldbank.org/indicator/NY.GDP.PCAP.CD

8. Kristalina Georgieva, "Remarks by Managing Director Kristalina Georgieva," *International Monetary Fund*, March 26, 2023, https://www.imf.org/en/News/Articles/2023/03/25/032623md-china-development-forum-remarks

CHAPTER 1

The Split

When I first moved to Tianjin, China, in 1997 to study Mandarin at Nankai University, friends back home wondered what I was doing. Why waste time learning Mandarin? "Go work for Goldman Sachs in New York," one friend said. Still reeling from sanctions enacted after the 1989 Tiananmen Incident, China was not considered a place for ambitious executives.

Eating meat regularly remained a luxury for many Chinese in those days—if you told anyone you thought China would become the world's largest retail market and power the sales of Louis Vuitton and BMW, they'd laugh in your face. Policymakers in DC thought it was a matter of when, not if, China's Communist Party would collapse and give way to a liberal democracy, the way the Soviet Union and communist regimes in Eastern Europe had fallen in the late 1980s.

What I saw on the ground in China as a student was completely different from the China I read about in *The New York Times* and *The Wall Street Journal*. Instead of finding a pessimistic population seething at Communist Party control, I found electric optimism coursing throughout the country. Chinese I interviewed felt the pragmatic reforms under Prime Minister Zhu Rongji would allow their children to have better lives than their own.

Within months of traveling around China, it became clear to me the country would hold great economic promise for American businesses which understood where policymakers were taking the country. Zhu and the Communist Party of China (CPC) wanted to promote economic integration with the rest of the world by adopting market-friendly policies while remaining true to socialism.

Before entering the business world, I wanted to learn as much as I could about China to eventually be a bridge between the US and China, so I pursued graduate studies at Harvard University focusing on China's political economy, studying under Professors Dwight Perkins, Liz Perry, and Samuel Huntington. I took a position as a teaching assistant for Professor William Kirby teaching Harvard undergraduates about China's modern history.

Wanting to get into the business world, I moved to Shanghai to work in venture capital in 2003. As I saw investment dollars flow into China, two years later I hung out my own shingle to help Western businesses and investors expand in China with a strategy consulting firm called the China Market Research Group (CMR).

I started my firm at the right time. Investing in China was all the rage after China entered the World Trade Organization (WTO) in 2001. Senior executives in fancy business suits descended on China to stay in gleaming newly built five-star hotels to scout out opportunities. They set up factories to take advantage of cheap labor, world-class infrastructure, and weak pollution regulations and eventually viewed China as a market to sell into.

Companies needed advice to navigate changing consumer behavior and political risk. I advised some of the world's leading companies and investors on their China strategies as consumers went from barely being able to put food on the table to powering sales of autos, luxury goods and semiconductors.

I have developed strategies for companies like Apple, KFC, DuPont, Crocs, Samsung, and Richemont, and conducted due diligence for Fidelity, Warburg Pincus, and other investors for billion-dollar investments—helping them earn billions in profits.

And profit American companies did. By the 2010s, China not only emerged as the world's factory, but it also became the world's largest retail market as double-digit economic growth turned hundreds of millions of peasants into middle-class consumers clamoring for Starbucks, KFC fried chicken, and Nike Air Jordans. Powered by middle-class and wealthy consumers, China emerged as the largest or second largest market in the world for most Fortune 500 companies.

China replaced America as the largest trade partner for over 120 countries.[1] Analysts predicted its economy would eclipse America's by the early 2030s. China's growth to superpower was inevitable.

After two decades of dizzying growth, instead of still seeing China as a weak nation on the verge of collapse, DC policymakers started to view China not only as economic but also a political and military threat to American dominance and the US-led rules-based world order. For its part, Beijing felt the "China Century" had arrived and that China would return to its rightful, dominant place in the world, as it had been before the collapse of the Qing dynasty at the hands of colonial powers in 1911.

In hindsight, it is almost inevitable a clash between the dominant superpower and the challenger with its different political, cultural, and value system would occur. National security advocates who believe China's rise threatens American national security caught the ear of an American president— Donald J. Trump—and shoved aside bridge builders like me who do not believe in zero-sum games.

Under Trump, free markets and globalization ran into a wall, and so did China's heady growth.

Rumblings of The Split

Until the Trump presidency, it was a no-brainer decision for American companies to invest in China—no country had the mix of rising incomes, scale, pro-business policies, and infrastructure that China possessed. Even with tension, American policymakers like George Bush Jr. and Barack Obama did not stop American companies from investing in China to seek profits. They wanted American companies to generate profits by benefiting from China's cheap labor pool and then by selling to those factory workers as they became middle-class consumers.

America's cozy business relationship with China hit a wall when Trump launched his trade war against China over what he called unfair trade practices and copyright infringement. Not wanting to look weak to foreign powers like the last emperors of the Qing dynasty did, Xi Jinping retaliated against Trump. China reduced purchases of American agricultural products like soybeans and beef and shifted supply chains to friendly countries like Brazil, South Africa, and Uruguay. From 2019 until 2023, Chinese airlines did not buy any Boeing jetliners, instead buying Airbuses from France.

Despite taking a hard line against Trump, China under Xi clearly wanted to reset relations and continue economic trade. In the run-up to the 2020 US presidential elections, China's foreign minister Wang Yi emphasized how China hoped for a return to relations built on mutual respect. China hoped Trump-era tensions and sanctions were a blip on what had been tense but generally good relations between China and the USA since the Mao Zedong–Richard Nixon era in the 1970s.

Within days of becoming president, however, Joe Biden dispelled China's dreams for rapprochement by doubling down on Trump's trade war. Biden launched what seemed to be never-ending economic sanctions on Chinese entities. Senior executives of global pension plans and school endowments told me the Biden regime pushed them in backrooms not to invest in China.

In response, the Chinese government became obsessed with national security, believing America was behind protest movements in Hong Kong and Xinjiang pushing for containment and regime change. Everywhere Beijing looked, they seemed to see spies. Newspapers and schools warned the population to be on the lookout for espionage.

China doubled down on efforts to root out spies and passed new cross-border data security laws under the guise of national security. The foreign business community bridled at new laws because of the high costs and worries executives could be arrested and held liable for minor infractions.

By the time Covid ended, China was no longer the must-invest destination it had once been. Senior executives and investors questioned whether China was still investable. Companies built up multiple supply chains, reducing the importance of China, and cut expectations for selling into China. Investors fled China's and Hong Kong's stock markets, reallocating toward Japan and India.

US media portrayals of China did not help—they hyped up risks, arguing China was becoming anti-business and anti-foreigner, adding to fears. Reports made it sound like innocent foreign executives were being arrested and detained arbitrarily simply for being foreigners.

US media, once again, does not portray China in a balanced manner. Although political risks are higher now than at any time since I arrived in China in 1997, China remains open for foreign business and is not arbitrarily arresting foreign executives. Since the end of Covid, senior officials from Prime Minister Li Qiang to Xi Jinping himself have launched a charm offensive on Western businesses in private meetings and in public conferences like at the Asia–Pacific (APAC) meetings in California.

China is arguably more open now to foreign investment than any time in the last 20 years. To jumpstart the economy after the end of zero-Covid, local governments rolled out the red carpet with free land and tax breaks to attract investment from foreign firms and eased visa policies for executives. Attracting foreign direct investment from large American companies is now one of the KPIs local officials are being measured against for promotion. One CEO of a division of a Fortune 500 American firm told me he built a factory in Zhejiang Province with local government money and that cities offered him 50 million RMB in tax subsidies to relocate his China headquarters to their city.

In other words, fears of China becoming un-investable for American businesses are overblown. In fact, even the most hawkish American policymakers do not want to end US–China trade completely.

Despite the rising tension between the US and China, it must be noted there is a difference between a Split and a complete decoupling. Even the Biden administration has stated China is too lucrative a market for most Western businesses to ignore, and it expects China to remain the world's factory. Katherine Tai, Biden's trade czar, said she does not see or want a total decoupling but wants to use the trade war as "leverage" to exact the best deals to benefit America.

Biden officials stopped using the term decoupling and now use the term *de-risking* to lower tension. Biden's ambassador to China, R. Nicholas Burns, said "divorce is not an option" because trade with China accounts for 750,000 American jobs and China buys one-fifth of American agriculture exports at 40.9 billion annually.[2] Aside from the most politically sensitive sectors where there are issues of national security, like semiconductors and artificial intelligence, America wants China to remain a major trade partner.

Despite the tension, decoupling won't happen unless there is a full-out war or if China invades Taiwan, leading America to sanction China like it did Putin's Russia, which is unlikely to happen in the near term. China has shown no major increase in battle preparations to attack Taiwan.

While foreign businesses face rising political risk and an economy facing structural headwinds, there is no other single market in the world that holds the potential for vast gains aside from perhaps India. However, India's per capita GDP remains about one-fifth of China's (2600 USD versus 13,160 USD). It will take years if not decades for India to catch up to China's economic might. Fast-growing countries like Vietnam and Saudi Arabia do not have China's scale, and Europe, as a whole, faces a lost decade due to Russia's invasion of Ukraine. Even if China adds 5 percent a year to its 19 trillion USD economy, that would be equivalent, as I said before, to adding an entire Thailand (520 billion USD) and Vietnam (370 billion USD) economy.[3]

In other words, the next China is China. To profit, businesspeople and investors need to understand how China's leaders are dealing with The Split. Initiatives like Xi's Common Prosperity will provide opportunities for companies who understand how the initiative will transform poorer regions like Hunan, Sichuan, and Xizang (Tibet) into economic powerhouses and double the size of the middle class. Other initiatives like China's Indigenous Innovation drive will help small Chinese technology players like those in the solar, NEV (new energy vehicle), and telecom sectors to innovate and emerge as global players, creating opportunities for investors and business partners.

Bridge building

Bridge builders on both sides of The Split need to forge peaceful relations that accommodate two superpowers or else the repercussions will be horrible. Former US secretary of state Henry Kissinger warned of a catastrophe worse than World War II if relations between the US and China deteriorate further. Billionaires Warren Buffett and Charlie Munger urged the US to "get along with China."[4] Bill Gates flew to Beijing where Xi Jinping welcomed him as an "old friend."[5] California governor Gavin Newsom said the US and China should not be seen to be in a zero-sum game and that both countries should cooperate and thrive.

In recent years, China has been aggressive in flexing its diplomatic and military muscles and deserves some blame for The Split. China should take a more conciliatory view in international affairs, especially when dealing with smaller countries like Australia, Lithuania, and the Philippines. It must reemphasize it wants peaceful reunification with Taiwan and must realize great powers should be beneficent and show restraint toward weaker nations. China should not launch trade wars and boycotts against small countries at the slightest hint of disagreement.

Despite deserved criticism of China, the greater part of the blame should be laid on American politicians and national security agencies like the FBI and CIA who fearmonger for votes and increased security budgets. Too many officials believe America should enforce imperialistic power over the rest of the world and are hellbent on turning China into an enemy. They are close to creating a self-fulfilling prophecy.

Republican Senator Ted Cruz from Texas said China has a 1000-year plan to destroy America. As outlandish as that sounds, South Dakota's governor Kristi Noem went farther and told Fox News "China has a 2000-year plan to destroy" America.[6] Florida governor Ron DeSantis banned Chinese nationals from buying property in Florida near military installations, after backing down from a blanket ban against Chinese nationals buying homes anywhere in Florida. Biden did little to calm the hysteria and Sinophobia by calling President Xi a "thug" and a "dictator."[7]

There are other underlying reasons for The Split. When the dominant superpower worries about losing power and influence to a rising superpower, it is natural for tension to occur. Pro-democracy zealots in America who are like the religious Crusaders of yore, like former US secretary of state Mike Pompeo, refuse self-determination and push for all nations to adopt American-style democracy are another reason for fraying relations. More darkly, racism, bigotry, and Sinophobia underscore the tension.

Conditioned by unbalanced US media portrayals and inflammatory rhetoric by politicians, everyday Americans worry China will try to enforce its political and value system on the rest of the world. China censors the media, limits religious freedom, and bans guns—all anathema to many Americans. Many Americans also worry that China is turning into a dictatorship under Xi Jinping, as Russia has under Putin, as decision-making has become centered around one man (Xi Jinping) more than any time in the post–Mao Zedong era.

The centralization of power around Xi has led to less risk taking among bureaucrats than in the post-1978 reform era, as officials only carry out explicit instructions from the top as they worry about getting punished for making mistakes. Foreign businessmen worry there are fewer checks and balances as well. For example, the new prime minister, Li Qiang, used to be Xi's advisor, and Cai Qi, the number five ranked party official in the standing committee of the Politburo, has been named Xi's chief of staff.

Despite the concentration of power around Xi, there is no reason to expect China to try to impose its political or value systems on other nations. It has not fired a single bullet in war outside of its borders from the 1980s onward nor has it instigated coups or regime change anywhere in the world. Xi's China is not like Putin's Russia. China continues strong relations with countries with democratic, communist and royal systems without criticizing those systems—in other words, it is plain hysteria to worry that Xi and China threaten the American way of life.

An aging growth playbook

China faces more economic challenges than at any time since I arrived in the country in 1997. Despite the constant doomsayers who have predicted China's economic implosion for decades, China has had a strong playbook to seek growth, attract foreign direct investment (FDI) to rely on manufacturing and the export sector, and invest in infrastructure and real estate.

The playbook worked so well because China started from a low base after the Cultural Revolution and the June 4th Tiananmen Incident. Following the playbook worked well, leading China's economy to become the second largest in the world with the world's largest retail market. American companies earned billions not only producing in China but also selling into it.

However, the playbook started to become outdated by the time Trump launched the trade war. Too much debt coursing through the real estate sector caused bubbles. China's largest real estate developer, Evergrande, went bankrupt. Local governments are heavily indebted from over investment into unsustainable infrastructure projects. China's famed cheap labor pool is fast disappearing as the population ages, as many young Chinese delay marriage or skip having babies completely.

In other words, there are simply not as many easy wins for the Chinese government to focus on anymore—the low-hanging fruit is gone. The government must return to its late 1990s ability under Zhu to move quickly, flexibly, and pragmatically to resolve structural challenges and find new growth drivers. The government must not be too beholden to inflexible ideological camps, get involved in geopolitical tussles, or become so obsessed with national security risks that they scare off foreign investors. China must go all-out in efforts to show the world China is open for business again.

The government has shown it recognizes the need for new growth drivers. They have supported indigenous innovation and the growth of new sectors like advanced machinery, NEVs, and a shift toward services. Making such a major shift is never easy. Worries over overcapacity abound. China's inevitably will face economic headwinds as it develops a new growth playbook.

What The Split means for businesses

Understanding the impact The Split has on businesses in different industries and countries is critical for business executives and investors to minimize risk and profit from the changes. Because of the geopolitical risk, it is no longer possible to say China overall is growing so we must invest there. Some foreign companies should invest in China; others should not.

This book is meant to be a guidebook for senior executives and investors trying to navigate the shifts and capture opportunities:

The first part of the book will look at the geopolitical and external pressures facing China and will analyze how The Split impacts sectors including artificial intelligence, semiconductors, rare earths, commodities like cotton and coal, and renewable energy. These chapters will look at how multinational firms and investors can navigate the tension to grab profits by launching new products and services or decide to cut back on exposure to China if the opportunities are limited.

To combat The Split, the Chinese government is promoting indigenous innovation and self-reliance. This part of the book will look at how investors can benefit as China tries to set new global standards in semiconductors, batteries, NEVs, and solar panels, what it calls New Productive Forces.

The second part of the book will look at internal pressures facing China from an aging economic growth model. To offset structural challenges, the government has turned toward socialism and ramped up patriotic drives. The government has focused on increasing the quality of life for poorer Chinese, who constitute 90 percent of the population, through initiatives like Common Prosperity and infrastructure spend to ensure a fairer playing field for all Chinese. The government has pushed to increase health care and education access for the 90 percent to unlock high savings rates and help them become middle class.

Conversely, initiatives like Common Prosperity limit the ability of wealthy Chinese, the 10 percent, to continue to get richer. Many are immigrating to other countries like Singapore or stopping investment because they are unsure of the domestic political winds. This section will show how brands need to alter marketing and sales strategies to target the 10 percent, whether in China or overseas.

The final part of the book will look at key Chinese consumer trends—how the spending habits of both the 10 percent and 90 percent are evolving in the post-Covid era, and how businesses and investors can capture the rise of the middle class to profit.

The last part of the book will look at trends among youth, female consumers, and the Silver Hair generation and how brands can target them. Youth are focusing more on health and spirituality. Female consumers are starting to become the main purchase decision-makers even for sectors like auto where men have traditionally dominated. The Silver Hair generation are immigrating or sending their children overseas to invest, creating opportunities for business globally to target the Silver Hair generation and their families.

Although China is no longer the no-brainer investment destination it once was, predictions of its demise are once again overstated. China is still investable even as it goes through rough times as the government replaces old drivers of growth with new ones.

It would be a mistake for multinationals and investors to ignore the world's second largest economy. It is true that not all businesses should invest in China anymore—the political risk is too high for many technology companies, for example—but for most businesses in less politically sensitive sectors, China should remain a major growth driver. This book provides a roadmap and framework for business executives and investors to understand the changes in China's political economy and how best to profit from those changes.

Notes

1. Mark Green, "China is the Top Trading Partner to More Than 120 Countries," *Stubborn Things,* Wilson Center blog, January 17, 2023, https://www.wilsoncenter.org/blog-post/china-top-trading-partner-more-120-countries
2. Nicholas Burns, Interview by Lesley Stahl, Aliza Chasan, Richard Bonin, and Mirella Brussani, *60 Minute Overtimes*, February 25, 2024, https://www.cbsnews.com/news/china-us-relationship-nicholas-burns-60-minutes/
3. World Bank, "GDP Per Capita," *World Bank Data*, https://data.worldbank.org/indicator/NY.GDP.PCAP.CD
4. Javier E. David, "Buffet and Munger Lash Out at 'Stupid': U.S.–China Tensions," *Axios*, May 6, 2023, https://www.axios.com/2023/05/06/berkshire-hathaway-annual-meeting-china
5. Michelle Toh, "China's Xi Greets 'Old Friend' Bill Gates in First Meeting with a US Business Magnate in Years," *CNN*, June 16, 2024, https://www.axios.com/2023/05/06/berkshire-hathaway-annual-meeting-china
6. Zhang Zhouxiang, "Creating an Anti-China Stage for Survival," Opinion, *China Daily*, March 17, 2023, https://global.chinadaily.com.cn/a/202303/17/WS6413a3f1a31057c47ebb4f13.html
7. Demetri Sevastopulo, "'This is a guy who is a thug': How US Elite Became Hawks on Xi's China," *Financial Times*, October 8, 2020, https://www.ft.com/content/75ce186e-41f7-4a9c-bff9-0f502c81e456

CHAPTER 2

The War for Artificial Intelligence Dominance

On a beautiful blue December day, I made my way along Beijing's bustling streets to meet with Deyu, the founder and CEO of a leading Chinese artificial intelligence (AI) company. With a runner's body, and a friendly, down-to-earth disposition, Deyu motioned me to sit as he poured me a cup of green tea. We were meeting to discuss the prospects for his business and how he could minimize rising political risk—from the American side.

Deyu's firm's shares had more than halved in the previous month on the Hong Kong Stock Exchange (HKSE). Investors worried his firm, and he personally, would be targeted and sanctioned by America, as Chinese tech giants like Huawei that America claimed posed national security risks had been. Deyu told me how his friend, a senior executive at another Chinese tech firm, had been ordered by the US to give up his green card or stop working for the Chinese firm.

As his firm's share price slid, Deyu borrowed to buy shares because the fundamentals of his business were sound, and revenue and profits were still rising. But because of what seemed to be a never-ending share price slide, he faced personal financial ruin as he was sitting on a loss of hundreds of millions of US dollars.

A sword of Damocles hung over Deyu's head, just like any founder of any Chinese technology company. Seemingly every month another Chinese firm gets sanctioned by America and the other member-countries of the Five Eyes security group—the UK, Australia, New Zealand, and Canada—which seem intent on stopping China's technological aspirations.

First came sanctions against telecom companies ZTE and Huawei under the Trump regime. Trump coerced countries from the UK to Australia to the Netherlands to ban Huawei products in their telecom networks. Former UK secretary of state for Business, Innovation and Skills during the Cameron administration, Vince Cable, revealed the US bullied the UK to ban Huawei, even though the intelligence and security services gave him assurances Huawei posed no risk.[1]

Biden banned American semiconductor firms from selling their newest technology to Chinese firms. Then came allegations TikTok, Tencent, and NEVs present national security risks. Congress released a report claiming ecommerce app Temu and fast-fashion retailer Shein, which had taken market share away from American companies like Amazon and Gap, were security risks and profited from using forced labor. Allegations in the report were littered with lots of possible, maybes, and potential risks but rarely if ever showed concrete evidence of actual national security risk breaches or forced labor.

Using security risks, claims of forced labor, or intellectual property infringement as the underlining reasons for the sanctions on China are red herrings—moves against Chinese tech firms are about controlling technology standards. Whoever controls the standards for the newest technology will continue to dominate.

Deyu worried he was next to be sanctioned, even though he has no connections with the military. He was scared the Americans would target him next simply because he runs an AI firm.

The threat of sanctions hung over Deyu's life's work, and he did not know what to do. He did not know how to navigate his company through increasingly treacherous waters to become a global player.

One of Deyu's board members, an Ivy League graduate, suggested splitting the company into two like Douyin did with TikTok—they'd split into a China-focused firm that Deyu would continue to run and an international one run by an American. The international company would separate from the China operations and raise capital from American financiers that DC could trust. The international company would house all data outside China to allay concerns from the American government that the CPC had access to data.

As he took a sip of tea, Deyu recounted to me his life story as if he was practicing what he would say if he faced a congressional grilling as TikTok CEO Shou Zi Chew did. If it was not for America, Deyu emphasized, he would never be as successful as he was.

Originally from one of China's poorest provinces, Deyu had taken a path that was the dream many a Chinese parent has for their children. Deyu secured a coveted job at an American technology firm about the same time I arrived in China to study Mandarin. In the Chinese sense, he had made it—a steady job, good salary, and a prestigious business card to pass out at conferences. But Deyu wanted more—he wanted to grab a pot of gold being made in the tech sector by fast-growing Chinese firms. In his early thirties, he left his steady job at the American technology firm to work at a high-flying Chinese tech start-up.

After a few years, Deyu saw fellow Chinese becoming billionaires as they started their own firms backed by venture capital money flowing in from Silicon Valley. Wanting to conquer the growing AI sector and grab an even bigger pot of gold, he set up his own company and searched for investors.

It was not hard for him to raise money. Billions of dollars of private equity investment flowed into China in those days. American venture capital firms, American pension funds like CalPERS and the New York State Pension Fund, and endowments from universities like Yale, Harvard, and Stanford poured billions into Chinese tech firms. Despite being portrayed as a Chinese firm beholden to the CPC, American private investors like General Atlantic, KKR, and Goldman Sachs control 60 percent of ByteDance, the parent company of TikTok.

The Chinese government did not stop American investors from investing in AI—in fact, the government encouraged American investment by doling out tax breaks. China wanted America's capital and tech know-how to help reform its economy away from low-end manufacturing. On the other side, American pensioners and students stood to profit handsomely if the bets on Chinese AI firms played out.

Deyu raised hundreds of millions of private equity money and became a beneficiary of the heady 2010s when investors rushed to find the next Alibaba. Revenues of Deyu's company grew fast, so he took his company public on the HKSE. After the initial public offering, the former peasant boy became worth several hundred million US dollars. Deyu became a media darling on Chinese television shows, invited to discuss his ground-breaking technology He embarked on a hiring spree and planned to expand internationally.

Unfortunately, the good times did not last long. First came China's crackdown on Jack Ma's Alibaba and the tech sector that sent Western investors fleeing the Chinese internet space. Investors worried Xi Jinping was anticapitalist and wanted state-owned enterprises (SOEs) to control new technologies due to his penchant for controlling everything.

Deyu was not concerned about the tech crackdown at all. He felt the crackdown provided him opportunities because Alibaba was monopoly-like and squelched innovation and fair competition. He believed the government cracked down to encourage smaller tech companies like his to grow. The government even pushed SOEs to buy his firm's products.

After the crackdown, Deyu kept appearing on state-owned television as the government wanted to showcase him as an example of indigenous innovation. Western investors still worried Deyu's firm would be caught up in the tech crackdown, so the share price kept collapsing. They did not understand the underlying reasons for the crackdown, Deyu believed—investors viewed it as a power play by Xi Jinping to control more aspects of Chinese society while Deyu viewed it as a way to ensure fair competition and spur innovation among start-ups.

Spooked Western investors reduced their exposure to China's tech sector and allocated capital to low-profile sectors, like bottled water, or simply exited all China investments. Funds switched allocations to Japan where policies seem more pro-business and decision-making transparent. As a billionaire hedge fund investor who had gotten burned as a tech sector investor told me, "China is dead. I won't invest there after the Alibaba crackdown. I lost too much money and can't trust what is happening regulatory wise."

Deyu asked me whether I thought he'd be sanctioned personally and what to do to prevent such a situation.

There was no easy solution to Deyu's problems. The threat of sanctions was very real, so he could either split his company into two, as ByteDance did with Douyin and TikTok, or bide his time and hope the political situation would get better.

Stuck between a rock and a hard place, Deyu became a casualty of US–China tension. Deyu's shares dropped

90 percent from its IPO price. No matter what Deyu did or said, investors viewed his company as too high a risk politically both from the American and Chinese sides, even though his firm continued to grow profits. In other words, political risk had essentially turned one of China's leading AI firms into a penny stock.

Many companies like Deyu's are getting caught in the crossfire of The Split. Biden's sanctions cause pain for China's technology sector in the short term as companies don't have access to America's newest technologies like semiconductors and share prices drop because investors fear they will be sanctioned.

Despite the short-term pain, in the long run, the bans will strengthen China's technology sector as Chinese players like Deyu's are forced to innovate and search for new revenue streams in new markets like the Global South rather than in America and Western Europe—if they do not, they will go out of business. The ones that can manage the shift will become more profitable than ever before.

The AI fight between democracies and autocracies

Even before OpenAI's ChatGPT and Sora stormed the world, AI had captured the attention of the business community more than any technology in the last decade. Unlike crypto and the metaverse, AI has proven business applications and profit models. It remains to be seen whether non-fungible tokens (NFTs) like Golden Apes are a short-term fad (most likely) or have staying power, or whether governments will crack down on cryptocurrencies after the collapse of Sam Bankman-Fried's fraudulent FTX. But AI already has applications which generate profits, from helping copyeditors and movie makers improve content, or responding to customer queries in online chats, to the Big Four accounting firms using AI to replace junior audit work. Just the rumor of a company being able to offer AI services sends share prices soaring.

Silicon Valley and China-focused venture capitalists have poured billions into the AI sector in search of the next Google or Alibaba. Chinese companies that can develop AI to sell to Chinese clients and to the Global South to streamline their business processes will grow huge profits. Futurists like former US presidential candidate Andrew Yang predict millions, if not billions, will lose their jobs to AI, much as factory workers lost their jobs to robots in the automation drive.

The fear over AI is not limited to workers worried about being replaced by algorithms. Venture capitalist Marc Andreessen argues the war for AI dominance is a moral one that will shape the world and determine the quality of our lives—Andreessen says the control for AI dominance is a war between just democracies like the US against autocracies like China.[2] America must win this war or else how Americans live their lives will be threatened Andreessen believes.

At the root of AI lies access to data and top semiconductor chips, made by American firms like Nvidia. China has the lead on data collection while the US leads on semiconductor innovation. Collecting data to be used in AI is a focus in boardrooms. Companies spend billions scraping data from the internet, collecting data from consumers and buying data from internet players. End consumers often are unaware their data is sold. Companies use AI to identify patterns in the data that can be used to push products or launch targeted marketing campaigns. AI is so good at analyzing consumer interest that watching a funny cat video on YouTube or Douyin now means opening the door to hyper-effective advertising of products and services that the algorithm predicts you want.

By the dawn of the Trump administration, America's military brass and national security agencies like the CIA became concerned China had taken the global lead in data collection as Chinese apps like TikTok and WeChat became popular globally. Worried Chinese tech companies would cooperate with the CPC to spy on Americans and collect data that could be used in AI applications by China's military to launch attacks, congressional representatives have tried to ban TikTok and other Chinese apps in America. The Democrat senator Mark Warner, chairman of the Senate Intelligence Committee, says parents should be "very concerned" about TikTok because it is an "enormous threat."[3] TikTok is already banned in India outright and on government mobile devices in the US and Australia.

There is some truth to the possibility Chinese tech companies collaborate with the Chinese government. Any mobile app, any device whether Chinese or not that connects to the internet, could theoretically be used by China's government to gain information to be used in AI. But the reality is that executives at Google, Tesla, and Microsoft have national security clearances because they work with America's military. Should China ban those companies outright from operating in China, too?

Instead of succumbing to hysteria and banning all Chinese apps, the US should reduce national security risks without hampering international trade. For example, it is possible medicine made in China could be intentionally tainted with toxins but that does not mean the US should stop the import of all antibiotics produced in China. Should HP's printers be banned simply because they are made in China? What about Apple iPhones made in China? Governments need to ensure good oversight without devolving to a 1950s McCarthy-style era of hysteria where all China-made products are deemed national security threats.

In America, a nexus of industry, academia, and weapons manufacturers has sounded the alarm about China's big data lead and potential AI strength and hyped the "China Threat." Aside from Andreessen, former Google chairman Eric Schmidt along with Harvard professor Graham Allison warned the US was on the verge of losing the AI war to China and that this is a "race the US can and must win" in the face of China's "autocracy."[4]

Criticism emerged that Chinese AI firms use facial recognition on millions of surveillance cameras set up around in a Big Brother–like attempt at control by police. Ominously, some activists allege cameras from HikVision input racial characteristics to track Uyghurs in order to oppress them. The Chinese government says tracking makes it easier to net criminals regardless of ethnicity, and does not target minorities. Law-abiding Chinese support the use of surveillance cameras for the most part and the use of facial recognition as they help police track down criminals. As one 39-year-old Shanghainese who owns a small hotel told me, "If you do not do anything illegal, you will support the use of cameras." Until the police deployed cameras, scammers commonly pretended to get hit by a car and demand payment.

American politicians should not exaggerate the threat of Chinese AI firms to American national security. In many ways, American hysteria is turning China into an enemy in a self-fulfilling prophecy by sanctioning Chinese firms and banning the sale of advanced technology to Chinese companies. Angry and frustrated at what they see as unfair policies and oppression, China is spending more on its military to protect itself.

The US should try to win the AI war by outcompeting China via fair competition through research and development. Innovations in AI will bring benefits to consumers and companies throughout the world.

Alas, taking a pragmatic and non-hysterical approach to China's rise is not happening in DC. America's politicians sanction China's tech sector, prevent the sale of advanced American technology to Chinese entities, and generally are trying to contain China's technological rise. Former US Secretary of the Treasury Lawrence H. Summers has decried the path American is taking to contain China's technological prowess. He says the US should focus on building up its strengths to compete with China rather than "tearing China down" with sanctions.[5]

Biden has not heeded Summer's criticisms. He has not only banned the sale of advanced semiconductors to China from American companies like Nvidia but threatened foreign tech companies like ASML and TSMC to make them stop selling to China.

Biden's sanctions went farther that just limiting semiconductor sales. Biden stopped American and US green card holders from advising and investing in Chinese chip firms to block American AI know-how going to China.

The Wall Street Journal found 43 American senior executives from 16 listed Chinese tech firms had to choose between their jobs and giving up American citizenships or green cards. Caught in the sanctions were Gerald Yin the chairman and founder of AMEC, a chip equipment manufacturer; Wayne Wei-Ming Dai, the CEO and founder of Verisilicon; and Stephen Kuong, the founder of Montage Technologies.[6]

In the short term, Biden's attacks will bring pain to China's economy but, in the long term, will strengthen it. The sanctions force China to build up its own technology supply chains. Biden has given China no other choice—develop its own tech industry or forever be forced to use older, inferior technology. Chinese companies are already overcoming sanctions rather than be crippled by them: Chinese semiconductor maker SMIC is catching up to US wafer technology, and Huawei has launched mobile phones without any American technology. Deyu's company is expanding into Southeast Asia. Not only do sanctions not stop Chinese firms from growing, but they also limit American firms like Qualcomm and Intel from being able to sell to the lucrative Chinese market.

Make no mistake—Biden intends to derail China's AI ambitions regardless of the cost to American businesses. US Secretary of Commerce Gina Raimondo announced she was willing to cut the profits of American companies by banning them from selling to China in order to secure America's national security.[7]

For its part, China's leadership believes whether China was communist or a liberal democracy, the US would not allow another country to threaten its dominance politically, economically, or technologically. Criticizing China for being communist, it believes, is a convenient way for American politicians to justify to Americans why it is oppressing China.

The world is seeing a reverse of the free-market economy and globalization push that lifted billions out of poverty after the collapse of the Soviet Union. No force has been better at poverty alleviation than economic globalization and fair competition. Ironically, the reverse is being led by America, which is supposed to stand for free markets and fair competition more than any other nation.

The growth of the Chinese AI ecosystem

Unless America ends sanctions, American and foreign technology companies from countries allied with the US like the

Netherlands and Japan cannot rely on the AI sector in China for growth. They are banned from selling their advanced technology to China by the US or run the risk of being banned in the future. Foreign technology companies can only sell inferior or outdated technology which Chinese companies do not want—they'd prefer to buy from Chinese suppliers, like chip company SMIC, that are moving up the value chain and which they trust will be able to provide years of steady supply.

It is simply not worthwhile for American tech firms to try to sell into China unless tensions ease. American tech companies should reduce their footprint in China and focus on selling into emerging markets like India and Vietnam that are supported by American politicians. What Biden is doing to contain China's AI and other tech ambitions is short-sighted and is shooting America in the foot. Not only is he destroying profit-making opportunities for American technology companies, but he is forcing Chinese competitors like Huawei and SMIC to innovate—Chinese players like Deyu's will eventually compete against American tech companies globally for market share. Nvidia already highlights Huawei as a competitor in chips after Huawei started to invest in R&D after being blocked from buying advanced chips from Nvidia. In other words, Biden has turned Huawei from Nvidia's client into its competitor.

Western investors can benefit by investing in Chinese technology firms in the AI space and in domestic suppliers in the AI supply chain. Instead of using American AI services like those from OpenAI or Google Gemini, Chinese firms will have to incorporate AI developed by Chinese firms like Deyu's into their operations. Investors should invest in the Chinese versions of OpenAI as well as the Chinese suppliers of semiconductors and other technologies critical for the development of AI. Although stock prices for Chinese AI firms like Deyu's have been hit by fears over being sanctioned by America and exaggerated worries over the political risk from the Chinese side, eventually investors will back firms like Deyu's as they continue to grow and profit within China and expand into the Global South.

Notes

1. "UK's Huawei Ban Driven by 'Selfish Political Gains': Chinese FM," *Global Times*, January 17, 2022, https://www.globaltimes. cn/page/202201/1246194.shtml

2. Marc Andreessen, "Why AI Will Save the World," *Andreessen Horowitz* blog, June 6, 2023, https://a16z.com/ai-will-save-the-world/

3. Emily Mae Czachor, "Warner Says White House Supports His Bill Targeting TikTok: 'One of My Bigger Fears' is How Data is Being Used by China," *Face the Nation*, CBS News, March 26, 2023, https://www.cbsnews.com/news/mark-warner-tiktok-white-house-supports-bill-bigger-fears-how-data-is-used-china-face-the-nation/

4. Eric Schmidt and Graham Allison, "Is China Winning the AI Race?" commentary, *Project Syndicate*, August 4, 2020, https://www.project-syndicate.org/commentary/china-versus-america-ai-race-pandemic-by-eric-schmidt-and-graham-allison-2020-08

5. Chris Anstey, "Summers Warns Very Risky for US to Aim at 'Tearing China Down,'" Interview with Larry Summers, *Bloomberg.com*, November 19, 2022, https://www.bloomberg.com/news/articles/2022-11-19/summers-warns-very-risky-for-us-to-aim-at-tearing-china-down

6. Liza Lin and Karen Hao, "American Executives in Limbo at Chinese Chip Companies After US Ban," *Wall Street Journal*, last modified October 16, 2022, https://www.wsj.com/articles/

american-executives-in-limbo-at-chinese-chip-companies-after-us-ban-11665912757

7. David Shephardson and Trevor Hunnicutt. "US Commerce Chief Heading to China with Aim of Boosting Business Ties," *Reuters*, August 25, 2023, https://www.reuters.com/markets/us-commerce-chief-heading-china-with-aim-boosting-business-ties-2023-08-25/

CHAPTER 3

War and the Battle for Rare Earths

"The Chinese are ten years ahead of the Americans when it comes to refining rare earths," Jordan, an Australian expert in rare earth told me over coffee in Shanghai. "Think of it this way," he explained, "the US is ten or even 20 years ahead of China in the semiconductor business. No matter how much the Chinese invest into semiconductors right now, they are still missing a lot of know-how that needs to go into the entire value chain."

Many people have heard of rare-earth elements (also known simply as rare earths) but are not really sure what they are used for or how important they are to the global economy. Because of their name, most people also think rare earths are rare in the sense that diamonds are and are hard to find. Despite the name, rare earths are actually not that rare. The 17 rare earths, which you can find on the periodic table, are found all over the world in mines and iron tailings from Brazil to Russia to Saudi Arabia. Being able to refine these tailings to make rare earths in a pure enough form to use in consumer electronics is what is elusive.

Rare earths are needed by our consumer-driven society as they power 7 trillion USD worth of consumer electronics from mobile phones to NEVs to microwaves. They also make the weapon systems for militaries deadlier and more accurate.

In other words, Jordan told me access to refined rare earth is just as critical as oil to a country's national interests and security. And look, he pointed out, at how many wars have been fought, coups launched, and vassal states and puppet regimes established over the demand to control access to oil supplies, from the Middle East to Africa to Latin America.

Considering the importance of rare earths, it is somewhat surprising that China managed to take control of the rare earth ecosystem without much protest from America and its allies: 85 percent of the world's refined rare earths come from China.[1] China accounts for 98 percent of Europe's rare earth supplies.[2] Imagine if one country controlled 85 percent of oil exploration and what that would mean for the global economy and political relations. To give context, Saudi Arabia controls 12.9 percent of the world's supply of petroleum, America 18.9 percent and Russia 11.9 percent.[3] American politicians pushed for shale oil exploration to end America's reliance on Saudi Arabia and other OPEC nations for its oil supply.

Yet, America surprisingly only recently started to push to end its reliance on China for rare earths. China has taken advantage of America's unpreparedness—China has developed technologies to refine rare earths that are years, if not decades, ahead of American technology.

Until recently, America was content with China dominating rare-earth refining. But with The Split reshaping political calculations and supply chains, American politicians are backing efforts to catch up to Chinese rare-earth refining capabilities. As American investors profited from the shift to shale gas in America, investors into rare-earth mining and refining facilities outside of Chinese control will also make huge profits.

In the same way it will take years for China to catch up to American, Dutch, and Taiwanese know-how in semiconductor innovation and manufacturing, it will take years for the US to catch up to China in mining and refining rare earths. But as determined as the Chinese are to catch up to America in semiconductor innovation, it is equally clear America is determined to catch up to Chinese dominance in rare earths. The race to secure rare-earth mines and refining capabilities provides opportunities for businesspeople to invest in rare-earth mines and refining technology and facilities outside of China in nations deemed friendly to America.

The history of rare-earth refining and pollution

China took the lead in rare-earth refining in the late 1970s and early 1980s when demand for rare earths expanded as consumer electronic giants like Sony, General Electric, and Siemens needed them as they started to sell television sets, phones, and refrigerators to middle-class households globally. Until the rise of the personal automobile, gasoline was worth very little. The same was true of rare earths. Until the consumer electronics revolution in the 1980s, rare earths held little value.

While governments started to recognize the economic potential from mining and refining rare earths and the need for them in weapon systems, they quickly found there was a downside to the mining and refining process—pollution. The runoff from the factories and mines poisoned rivers and entire wildlife ecosystems. Developed countries like the US and European nations did not want to mine or refine rare earths because of the high costs to the environment, so they sought to buy rare earths from countries willing to do so despite the pollution.

China, desperate for capital and job creation after the Cultural Revolution ended in 1976, gladly became the main source for rare earths globally regardless of the pollution.

Relations between the US and China had just been reestablished during the Nixon era, and a heady wave of cooperation had started. China was so poor the US did not view it as a military threat. America was fine with China dominating such a high-polluting industry. President Ronald Reagan worried more about the Soviet Union and Japan as threats to American dominance than China. Policymakers under Reagan and, later, Presidents George H. W. Bush and Bill Clinton also believed the CPC would inevitably collapse and be replaced by a liberal democracy that would be an American ally as soon as China's middle class emerged and demanded more political say. For those planners, it was not a long-term risk to have China, even if it was communist, control an important but in those days not a mission-critical sector.

American and European politicians also did not predict the pace of technological innovation in the coming decades and how consumer electronics would become integral to daily life in the 21st century. In those days, computers were often the size of a room, so politicians did not expect every person would one day tote around multiple electronic devices like mobile phones and laptops. For government officials, while securing access to rare earths was important, it was not as critical as ensuring access to oil.

China soon dominated the refining of the rare earths that were needed by households around the world to run the consumer electronics that make life comfortable. As the consumer electronic revolution became a reality, this meant China controlled commodities every bit as important as oil. American and European policymakers started to worry China controlled rare earths. If Western powers wanted to de-risk from China, they would also have to end their reliance on China for rare-earth supplies.

A new arms race

Aside from a consumer electronic revolution, military planners began to realize the importance of rare earths for national defense. Despite the rise of artificial intelligence, as Vladimir Putin has shown in Russia's invasion of Ukraine or Benjamin Netanyahu in the Israeli bombing in Gaza, conventional wars are not part of a bygone era—wars will still be fought through weapons that kill and maim. Rare earths are needed for those weapon systems.

As America and her allies become more concerned about China's growing power and what they call its aggressiveness over Taiwan and in the South China Sea, governments have embarked on an arms race to deter China in an era of tension not seen since the 1930s.

American politicians like Mitt Romney and Lindsey Graham have backed over 100 billion USD in weapon sales to Ukraine, Israel, and Taiwan to defeat Russia and to "deter China." American politicians say, if America doesn't stop Russia in Ukraine, then China will invade Taiwan. *The Economist*'s editor-in-chief Zanny Minton Beddoes argues that arming Ukraine is the cheapest way for America to ensure its national security without having Americans die. Japan has announced it will double its military spending in the next five years over worries over China's rise.

As nations embark on an arms race, countries who control rare-earth mining and refining will wield the same power as those who control oil and semi-conductors. China's near monopoly on rare earth refining gives it leverage over other nations. As China's former leader Deng Xiaoping once said, "The Middle East has oil. China has rare earths." The battle to secure rare earth supplies with be critical for nations in their moves to shore up self-defense and de-risk from China.

Forgetting the horrors of war

Humans unfortunately have the ability and habit to devise different ways to hurt their fellows. From cavemen shaping spears out of rock to J. Robert Oppenheimer developing the atom bomb, conflict and war have been the few consistent things in human history. Today, hundreds of millions of our fellow humans suffer privation from war on a daily basis due to racism, bigotry, and the base pursuit of power by many of the world's political leaders.

Breaks in warfare happen only when the people and their political leaders have suffered too much and clamor for peace. This happened to politicians in Europe who remembered the devastation of World War I and World War II and created the European Union to bind together former enemies and integrate economies to minimize the risk of war breaking out again. Some Western politicians are forgetting those lessons and, according to NATO's secretary general, Jens Stoltenberg, are expanding NATO's purview to cover not just Europe but also Asia, with an eye on China.[4] Germany's Green Party has been especially critical of China, as has Ursula von der Leyen, the president of the European Commission and former minister of defense for Germany.[5]

Under Stoltenberg, NATO announced it was considering opening a liaison office in Japan, causing concern in Beijing at NATO's expanding remit. In the meantime, weapons manufacturers like Raytheon and Lockheed Martin are seeing share prices soar as America sells more weapons to allies like Ukraine, Australia, and Taiwan. AUKUS, a trilateral security pact between Australia, the UK, and the USA will see America sell tens of billions of US dollars' worth of nuclear-powered submarines to Australia.

In China, senior government officials in the late 1970s to late 2010s did anything to maintain peace and stability, often being conciliatory in international affairs in order to keep the peace. Chinese leaders like Deng Xiaoping and Ye Jianying suffered privations, desperation, and degradations stemming from World War II, the Chinese Civil War, and the Cultural Revolution. During the Deng Xiaoping, Jiang Zemin, and Hu Jintao eras, peace and stability and getting food on the tables of their people trumped all else.

In China today, many of those lessons to do anything to avert war are starting to be forgotten as well, as China spends more on its military capabilities to safeguard its interests against the US, NATO, and an increasingly militant Japan. Xi wants to project a strong China that will not back down and look weak, lest China suffers another hundred years of humiliation at the hands of Western powers. Like American weapon manufacturers Lockheed Martin and Raytheon, Chinese weapon manufacturers like Norinco have benefited from Russia's war with Ukraine, selling throughout Africa, grabbing market share from Russian weapon manufacturers that have had to abandon exports in order to arm Russian and Wagner forces fighting Ukraine.

America, on the other hand, due to its geographical location and warm ties with immediate neighbors, Canada and Mexico, has not dealt with war on its soil in over 150 years. While America has seemingly been perpetually at war since its founding—only for 21 years since its founding in 1776 has the US not been engaged in war—its citizens have never had to deal with the horror of the bombings of its cities from foreign forces.[6] Relative peace has left American politicians and the greater population gung-ho. War to them is a far-off occurrence.

The coming decade will see an arms race as politicians throughout the world forget their history lessons. Everyday humans will suffer, but investors in rare earths, and weapons companies, will benefit.

China's dominance in rare-earth refining

To learn about the rare-earth refining process, I arranged a visit with Mr. Wang at one of China's rare-earth factories. Mr. Wang had been instrumental in building the rare-earth refining facilities for several of China's largest state-owned enterprises (SOEs).

Although the Chinese state controlled most refineries, a few private entrepreneurs with strong military connections set up facilities in the late 1990s before the government stopped issuing licenses in rare earths to the private sector. Until President Jiang Zemin banned the Chinese military from taking direct stakes in companies, it was common for well-connected individuals (often relatives of generals) to open up companies and give the military a stake. Military corruption has long been one of China's weak spots as it has limited its military preparedness, which is why Xi arrested many of China's top brass including Generals Xu Caihou and Guo Boxiong, both former vice chairmen of the powerful Central Military Commission.

As China's political leaders realized the importance of rare earths for weapons and ensuring national security, there has been a push for state-owned enterprises to take over private facilities. It is likely that number of private refineries will drop further as Xi focuses on national security.

Mr. Wang shook my hand and waved toward the silos towering behind him. As we walked toward the refinery, Mr. Wang first showed me large bags of dirt with labels from different countries. He explained that the factory bought iron-ore tailings from mines around the world, from Latin America to Africa to Russia, and brought them to the factory to process. Echoing Jordan, Mr. Wang explained that rare earths were not that rare but that the refining process developed by Chinese factories were able to extract more value out of iron-ore tailings than factories in Australia and America.

As we entered the factory, I could see hot liquids of different dark and light hues bubbling through row after row of transparent pipes, flowing from one cauldron to another. The factory floor was mostly automated.

Mr. Wang told me that, over the decades, China had spent so many resources innovating that China now produced the best rare-earth refining machines. He said China could refine rare earths to a purer form, and extract more from the raw materials, than any other country in the world.

Mirroring Jordan's views, Mr. Wang believed Chinese rare-earth technology is decades ahead of that of any other country in the world. He said the US and Australia would have to spend billions of dollars and many years, if not decades, to catch up.

China's lead in rare-earth refining gives China leverage over Europe and America and serves as a weapon of last resort— China can shut off the taps to the world's consumer economy. Shutting off the taps would be a weapon of last resort, like a nuclear weapon, but gives China enormous leverage.

As we walked through the refinery, Mr. Wang showed me an area that collected the plant's polluted waste. Ten years ago, pollution had been a problem in refineries. But, under Xi, the government has developed strict pollution standards, even in rare earths, so today China's refineries are held to the highest environmental standards. Indeed, the area around the factory was beautiful, in the middle of what looked like a nature reserve. This was not the dirty, high-polluting factory that I had expected to see.

A worried America and what this means for investors

China's lead in rare-earth refining has rightly worried American military planners. Were war to break out, China could simply stop exporting rare earths to the US and its military would immediately be unable to produce advanced weapons and defense systems. Imagine what would happen if America's tanks and fighter jets no longer had access to gas to power their engines. Unlike China's dominance in manufacturing where risks are exaggerated, China's stranglehold on rare earths does pose a risk to American national security.

As a result, the US Department of Defense is trying to secure access to rare-earth mines and refineries. They have bought huge stakes in Australian refinery Lynas and are searching for new mines and refineries around the world.[7] Even with new investments, America still lags far behind China's refining capabilities.

For America, Europe, and countries not politically friendly with China, there are risks to China's control of the rare-earth industry. If China ever feels cornered by provocations, they could turn off the export of rare earths, causing that nation's economy to stall. China has done this before: in 2010, it turned off the export taps to Japan after that country's detention of a Chinese fishing trawler captain. Limiting exports of rare earths to a country would be like OPEC suddenly banning all exports of oil to other countries—the inflation and impact on economies could be devastating, causing shortages, runaway inflation, and social instability.

China retaliated against Biden's technology sanctions by demonstrating its power over the rare-earth sector and launching export controls on gallium and germanium. Chinese exporters now need permission from the Chinese government to export to the US—some months, no permissions are given as a warning to the US. These new export controls have caused shockwaves through the defense departments of countries around the world. Corporate officers worry they would no longer be able to make the consumer electronics that consumers demand if they did not have access to Chinese gallium. While China has not outright banned the export of gallium, they have forced permission to be granted before it can be exported as a shot across the bow to other nations like the US not to go too far in implementing sanctions on China. It is no coincidence that Vietnam announced it would go into rare-earth refining the month after China's germanium and gallium controls came into effect.

Rising geopolitical tension and China's threats to block rare-earth exports from China has forced America and Europe to search for new sources of refined rare earths. Countries and factories that can replace China's importance in the rare-earth ecosystem will generate great windfalls.

Securing access to refined rare earths outside of China

Like artificial intelligence and semiconductors, rare earth will be the next battleground for control by the world's governments that will cause a split in supply chains. In the coming decades, there will be a battle to control rare-earth supplies and refining capabilities. Not having access to rare earths poses too large a risk for militaries and companies—relying so much on China for their rare-earth needs is a risk that America and her allies cannot afford.

Governments will need rare earths to equip their militaries, and consumer electronic companies like Siemens and Apple will need to secure long-term access to rare earths. The consumer electronic revolution and arms race means there are profit opportunities for companies and investors that can secure access to rare-earth mines and develop the refining process outside of China. Within China, the sector will face headwinds as they will face increased international competition from American-backed players. Chinese state-owned and private players will face more international competition and shrinking margins domestically in China as the government exerts more oversight in such a key sector. It is likely that private rare-earth companies will be forced to sell to state-owned enterprises in the name of national security.

Notes

1. Milton Ezrati, "How Much Control Does China Have Over Rare Earth Elements?" *Forbes.* December 11, 2023, https://www.forbes.com/sites/miltonezrati/2023/12/11/how-much-control-does-china-have-over-rare-earth-elements/?sh=58dc70605b21#:~:text=According percent20to percent20a percent20study percent20from, earthpercent20deposits percent20in percent20Chinese percent20 territory

2. Polish Economic Institute, "98 percent of EU Demand for Rare-Earth Elements is Met by China," *Polish Economic Institute,* online article, June 9, 2023, https://pie.net.pl/en/98-of-eu-demand-for-rare-earth-elements-is-met-by-china/#:~:text=As percent20much

percent20as percent2098 percent25 percent20of,niobium percent 20it percent20consumes percent20from percent20Brazil

3. Pallavi Rao, "Ranked: The World's Biggest Oil Producers," *Visual Capitalist*, September 23, 2023, https://elements.visualcapitalist. com/ranked-the-worlds-biggest-oil-producers/

4. Charles Szumski, "Stoltenberg warns business world on China," *Euractiv*, December 9, 2022. The Capitals, https://www.euractiv. com/section/politics/news/stoltenberg-warns-business-world-on-china/

5. Gabriel Bub, "Diplomacy: How Macron woos Xi while von der Leyen makes threats," *Table Media*, May 6, 2024, China, https://table.media/en/europe/feature-eur/macron-ensnares-xi-while-von-der-leyen-threatens/

6. Christina Oord, "Believe It or Not: Since Its Birth the USA Has Only had 17 Years of Peace," *War History Online*, March 19, 2019, https://www.warhistoryonline.com/instant-articles/usa-only-17-years-of-peace.html

7. Praveen Menon and Riya Sharma, "Australia's Lynas Gets $120 mln Pentagon Contract for U.S. Rare Earths Project," *Reuters*, June 15, 2022, https://www.reuters.com/markets/us/australias-lynas-secures-120-mln-pentagon-contract-us-rare-earths-facility-2022-06-14/

CHAPTER 4

Indigenous Innovation

The Battle for Semiconductor Dominance

"My business is booming!" said a slightly doughy Tsinghua graduate named Frank, beaming at me. Like many top Chinese students he told me he went to graduate school in the US in the mid-1990s because he thought there were better opportunities there than in China in those days.

After graduation, the opportunities in China were only for the adventurous, entrepreneurial type so the risk-averse Frank stayed in America and worked for a leading semiconductor firm. For ten years, he lived the dream. He bought a house with a backyard and a car—a luxury only for the very rich in China in the 1990s. He got married and gave birth to two kids who took American citizenship. He was content living in California until he saw his classmates who had remained in China get rich in start-ups in the 2000s. Frank decided to leave America and relocate his whole family back to China to start his own semiconductor firm. Like Deyu, he wanted to get rich and grab a pot of gold.

"The first few years of entrepreneurship were tough," Frank told me. He said he was often outcompeted by European and America suppliers because they had better technology. He sold to Chinese customers who were looking for cheap but good enough.

Frank's fortunes changed literally overnight after Trump's sanctions on telecommunications multinational Huawei. Huawei called him and switched its supply chain from foreign technology providers to Chinese domestic suppliers like Frank's company. Frank's business soared: "We can't keep up with the orders. Our factories are running 24/7." Even if his firm's technology was not as good as American equivalents, it didn't matter—Chinese companies could rely on him to provide a steady supply of equipment. And his firm was slowly improving its technology and would soon catch up to American quality.

Frank told me he was waiting for approval for his company to go public on the A-share market China. Once he had raised the capital, he would deploy millions, if not billions, to R&D and finally catch up to American technology players.

Rather than destroy Huawei and China's technology sector at large, sanctions on semiconductor exports to China have actually forced the government and private companies to cooperate and invest in R&D in areas where they previously would have been comfortable relying on American or European suppliers. Until the doubling down on sanctions by Biden, for most Chinese companies it was not worth the investment or R&D costs for most companies. They could just buy American technology. The sanctions created opportunities for Chinese tech players to evolve from being cheap but good enough to rivalling American and European players in innovation. Entrepreneurs like Frank benefit from The Split. Companies like his in China's semiconductor technology supply chain are thriving—not dying—thanks to Trump's and Biden's myopia.

Focus on self-reliance

American sanctions on China's technology sector, as we saw in the previous chapter on artificial intelligence, have made it imperative for China to focus on self-reliance. The government has pushed for domestic companies to focus on innovation and has ploughed tens of billions of US dollars into R&D to support them. Moreover, as part of the search for a new growth model, the government subsidizes sectors like NEVs, rechargeable batteries, advanced machinery, and solar panels to create national players that set global standards and replace the real estate sector as drivers for growth.

Foreign investors can profit by backing public national champions. Chinese NEV maker BYD, for example, eclipsed Tesla to become the largest NEV maker in the world—BYD has established sales operations all over Southeast Asia, the Middle East, and Europe, undercutting legacy automakers like Volkswagen and Toyota on price and innovation and threatening their market share. In an act of protectionism, America made Chinese NEVs subject to a 100 percent tariff so it is unlikely Americans will see cheap Chinese NEVs anytime soon.

Despite criticism from Congress, American auto giant Ford has tried to set up a joint venture with Chinese battery manufacturer CATL because the Chinese have the best battery technology in the world. In the entire ecosystems of sectors backed by Beijing to become new growth drivers, Chinese players and their foreign partners will see huge profits.

For Chinese policymakers, the focus on indigenous innovation in semiconductors and other key areas like batteries where China can control global standards is a do-or-die situation, or else China's economy will face decades of economic stagnation. Beijing only has to look to Japan to see what happened to Japan's economy when it rivaled America in power in the 1980s. America sanctioned Japan's semiconductor and other tech ambitions, causing it to enter a multi-decade stagnation because it failed to focus on sectors to innovate in to spur economic growth.

Learning from history

By the mid-1980s, Japan's manufacturing electronics giant Toshiba was set to surpass in Silicon Valley to lead the world in semiconductor innovation. Known as the foundation of technology, semiconductors power computers, mobile phones, and NEVs. Without semiconductor chips from Nvidia, artificial intelligence would not have been created and the satellite systems GPS and Beidou would remain figments of the imagination. Microscopic in size, semiconductors are the single most complicated thing ever produced by humankind.

In our age of technology, whoever controls the semiconductor sector controls the technology supply chain and stands dominant in world power. Ever since the rise of computing, it was American firms like Intel, Nvidia, and Qualcomm that led innovation, giving America leverage over other nations. America could stop exporting chips to cripple the technology sectors of adversaries. While China has rare earths and the Middle East oil, America controls semiconductors.

Having a Japanese firm like Toshiba threaten to outcompete America in semiconductor advancement was an affront to American power and prestige. Other Japanese firms had already taken away share from American industrial giants, threatening the core of American economic dominance. Cars from Japanese auto makers Toyota and Nissan flooded the

US market, "stealing" market share from once-dominant American auto firms General Motors and Ford. Sony's Walkman and televisions grabbed market share away from American companies like General Electric (GE). By the 1980s, Japan rivalled and arguably surpassed the US in innovation and quality control in consumer electronics and autos.

This, combined with a weak yen that made Japanese exports cheaper than America's, enabled Japanese companies to begin dominating global manufacturing. Not only did Japan make cheap but good enough products, but it had become innovative and created great brands. Japanese firms used their profits to buy up iconic American real estate like New York City's Rockefeller Center and the Pebble Beach Golf Links, California.

Fear rose in DC and boardrooms that America's power and influence would be surpassed by its World War II enemy. War hawks worried the American-led world order in place since the 1940s would be undermined and that Japan would threaten the American way of life. Instead of pushing American industry to outcompete Japan with investment into R&D, America alleged Japan played unfairly. American officials called Japan an aggressor, intellectual property (IP) infringer, and currency manipulator that threatened American national security, much as politicians now call China an aggressor, IP infringer, and currency manipulator. American politicians pushed for sanctions and other economic coercive measures to stop Japan's ascent.

The criticism of China's values today by Australian prime minister Scott Morrison and US secretary of state Antony Blinken mirror the criticisms of Japan's values in the 1980s. Government officials across the political spectrum in America like former Speaker of the House Democrat Nancy Pelosi and the Republican senator Tom Cotton from Arkansas also paint China's value systems as lower and immoral, not just different.[1] The message is very clear—America with its democratic ideals is the global moral standard bearer while red communist China holds an inferior value system.

Worried about Japan's ascent, President Reagan pushed Japan to appreciate the yen, causing its exports to sputter and curtailing the country's semiconductor ambitions. After the Plaza Accord of 1985, exports from Japan to the US halved between 1986 and 1992 because prices were too high. Japanese real estate prices crashed and even three decades later had not recovered. It took 30 years for Japan's equity markets to retouch their highs of the 1980s.[2]

Many attribute Japan's subsequent decades of economic stagnation to US efforts to contain Japan's semiconductor innovation and exports.[3] Reagan neutered Japan's ability to be a leader technologically and globally in the world in the sectors that count—the US was fine with Sony selling commodity-like televisions and CD players but would not allow Japanese firms like Toshiba to sit at the top of the semiconductor supply chain and set global standards. Reagan slapped a 100 percent tariff on Toshiba's products before eventually banning Toshiba from selling into the US for five years.

Looking at Japan's experiences, China's leaders concluded the US wanted to contain Japan in the 1980s because it was outcompeting it on technology and in manufacturing, Beijing sees parallels with the sanctions America is placing on China today. They believe Congress wants to contain and cripple China's economy with literally the same accusations and allegations levied against Japan. America was fine with Sony making televisions, just as it is OK with Chinese consumer electronics makers like Xiaomi and TCL making televisions, but it is not OK with the Chinese taking the lead in telecom or semiconductor innovation—the technologies that count.

Chinese policymakers have concluded they cannot follow Japan's path—they must support indigenous innovation in semiconductors and not to become too dependent on foreign technology. They also cannot appreciate the RMB too much and cause Chinese exports to become too expensive. In other words, China cannot bow down to American might like Japan did and sign any accords that will hurt China's ability to innovate and remain a manufacturing powerhouse

A Japanification of China's economy

China's weak economy in the post-Covid era has led analysts to argue China faces a Japanification of its economy where decades of economic stagnation is inevitable because of an aging population and heavily indebted real estate sector. While there are certainly similarities, China's economy will remain robust because there are key differences between how China will respond to American containment policies.

Unlike Japan, China will not back down and agree to this century's version of the Plaza Accord. It won't curb its technology ambitions or appreciate its currency, the yuan. It will continue to support a start-up ecosystem and push to remain the world's factory. It also has a population, ten times larger than Japan's, that wants to buy foreign products.

Japan capitulated to the US in part because there were 50,000 American GIs stationed on Okinawa, effectively occupying the country. Japan bowed down to Reagan's demands because it had little choice. China is different. There are no American troops stationed in China.

Many of Japan's politicians also enjoy tacit and implicit backing from the US and are part of family political dynasties that have cooperated with America for generations. For example, the assassinated prime minister Abe Shinzo was the maternal grandson of former prime minister Kishi Nobusuke who was imprisoned as a suspected "Class-A" war criminal for crimes committed in China during World War II. America released him. He later became prime minster and forged strong relations with America. Abe's father, Abe Shintaro, was the former minister for foreign affairs who also enjoyed tight relations with DC.

Conversely, China under Xi won't back down. Xi does not need or enjoy backing from the US as a root of his power. Xi has touted to the Chinese population that China has its own strong political system—Marxism with Chinese characteristics that is also a democracy (isn't that a mouthful?)—that won't bow down to any other country. Schoolchildren are taught the country suffered a century of humiliation to Western powers. The Chinese population would not accept Xi giving in to American demands.

Moreover, Japan's economy has been dominated by the remnants of the old *keiretsu* (groups of companies with shared business interests and often familial ties) like Mitsubishi, which prevent a flourishing start-up culture. China, on the other hand, has a vibrant ecosystem of technology entrepreneurs like Deyu and Frank—after the tech crackdown on Alibaba and Tencent, as we shall see in Chapter 6, no single corporation that is not controlled directly by the government wields as much power in China as the old *keiretsu*.

None of China's most senior leaders in the post–20th People's Congress era spent considerable time abroad as Japanese politicians have. None has longstanding relations with foreign counterparts. Most moved up the ranks after working in provincial roles. Premier Li Qiang is the first premier in decades not to have served as a vice premier before becoming premier—previous premiers Zhu Rongji, Wen Jiabao, and Li Keqiang had all previously served as vice premiers before taking the premiership. Because of Covid border lockdowns, as they rose through the ranks of the Communist Party, China's current leaders did not get the chance to forge close relations with senior counterparts from America and other nations. Ultimately, they owe their positions to Xi's patronage.

All seven members of China's standing committee of the Politburo were also all teenagers or in their twenties during the Cultural Revolution when they learned out of necessity how to be strong for self-preservation to ward off the chaos the Red Guards unleashed on the country. They won't back down like Japan's rulers did—they are more likely to push back to demonstrate power, which they learned to for do self-preservation during the Cultural Revolution. They are more likely to exaggerate China's power than to "hide your strength, bide your time," as former Chinese leader Deng Xiaoping once famously stated.

Instead of backing down on technological innovation as Japan did, China has doubled down on research and development to support indigenous innovation through the establishment of private equity funds and subsidies and forcing SOEs to buy technology from private Chinese firms like Deyu's. Allocating tens of billions of dollars to the policy, the government has pushed for state-owned enterprises and private Chinese firms like Tencent and Alibaba to cooperate in making semiconductor development a priority. Chinese semiconductor companies like Hua Rong and SMIC are catching up to American technology quickly and have seen market share grow as companies like Huawei are forced to rely on their products rather than foreign ones. Companies in the Global South have also seen how the US has sanctioned China and worry they, too, will one day be sanctioned for human rights abuses or for not adhering to American hegemony, and so are buying more Chinese technology from companies that do not come with the same political strings attached.

Self-reliance—a long-term goal

Contrary to many China watchers who blame a paranoid and warmongering Xi for pushing self-reliance, China's focus on indigenous innovation was actually in place even before Xi Jinping became chairman. Indigenous Innovation was a policy started in 2006 during the Hu Jintao administration when the Ministry of Science and Technology, National Development and Reform Commission, and Ministry of Finance issued the "Method for Determining the National 'Indigenous Innovation,'" which became law in 2009.[4]

Having seen what happened to Japan, China's government has long been concerned about being held hostage to the US over technology access and also wanted to become a power in technology where profit margins and influence are higher. Even in those days when China was still far from being an economic superpower, China did not want simply to be the world's factory for cheap toys and clothes. They had ambitions to become a global superpower as it had been before the fall of the Qing dynasty (1636–1911).

To support local industry, for decades China's central government often directed state-owned enterprises and government ministries to replace American software and hardware whenever possible with local Chinese options. There have long been worries US technology giants could send data back to the CIA. Rumor had it that China's military bases banned Tesla cars from entering their compounds because of fears the CIA could use the onboard cameras to beam back secrets and coordinates to the US military.

Rising political tension and fears over national security have caused problems for American technology companies looking to expand in China. An American software company in the SaaS (software as a service) sector engaged my firm, CMR, to develop a strategy to sell to state-owned enterprises, once one of their largest target markets, after their SOE clients suddenly dropped them. The prognosis was not good, we found, as the central government pushed for the adoption of software from Chinese players because of data and national security concerns. We found our client could still sell to local governments which had their own budgets and procurement processes, just as Bill did (as we saw in the Preface). Local governments focused more on hitting GDP growth targets and were less worried about national security issues. But many local governments have become wary of buying foreign technology after being burned, like Bill, when American firms suddenly stopped projects over fears of being sanctioned. Selling to the central government, and even to state-owned enterprises, is difficult, as here national security concerns trump profit goals. We told our client it would be better to focus on selling to Chinese private enterprises rather than government affiliated entities.

America's long arm of sanctions has hit not just American but also the ability of European and Asian technology firms to profit. The Dutch and Japanese governments acquiesced to American pressure to ban advanced semiconductor sales to Chinese entities even if it hurt their companies. A senior executive of a Dutch semiconductor firm brainstormed with me on what to do with his China operations. Because of

American sanctions, his company was no longer able to sell his most advanced technology to Chinese clients. He used the term "American bullying" to express his anger at his lost revenue. Chinese companies worry that Europe, Japan, and other American allies will eventually launch export controls so it is safer for them to buy from Chinese suppliers.

Until heightened tensions from the Trump era, private Chinese firms often ignored Chinese government directives and concerns and utilized American technology as the underlying core of their businesses. Why spend years and billions in research when companies could simply buy Intel semiconductors and operating systems like Google's Android and still make money by selling mobile handsets to Chinese consumers at a fraction of Apple's price? Until Trump, few Chinese firms focused on technological innovation—they just took what worked in America and applied it for China specifically. They utilized American technology to focus on business model innovation to improve manufacturing efficiency and keep prices to customers low. The strategy worked, as proven by soaring sales and skyrocketing stock prices.

It was only after Trump sanctioned Huawei that Chinese firms started to realize the precarious position they were in by not controlling the underlying technology. Without American 5G technology and Google's Android operating system, Huawei's mobile phone sales plummeted almost overnight. Huawei regained market share in the handset business only after launching its own operating system years later, which is now deployed on over 200 million devices, and relying on Chinese suppliers.

Having seen Huawei's handset business decimated by Trump, other Chinese firms started to invest full force in indigenous innovation, backed by government directives and money. If even such an innovative giant as Huawei with access to capital and government support could be damaged by American sanctions, Chinese entrepreneurs realized their own companies were at risk. Innovation and procuring from Chinese suppliers have become a matter of do-or-die. They have focused on innovation and selling good enough technology at cheaper rates to countries in the Global South like Saudi Arabia that are looking for good prices and which are also concerned about American imperialism.

China's potential to rival America as technology provider to Asia and the rest of the Global South is aided by the fact that it never invaded other countries like Japan did during World War II. While there is undoubtedly hesitation and anxiety about China's rise by its neighbors in Asia, especially in South Korea, Japan, and India, there is not the same fear and hate throughout Asia directed toward Japan due to its atrocities committed during World War II. China's neighbors like Indonesia, Thailand, and even Vietnam are willing to buy Chinese technology—they just want the best technology at a good price to help their populations enrichen themselves.

China has become the largest trade partner of nearly every country in Asia, and is viewed as not trying to export or foist its political system onto other countries as the US does. For many countries in Asia, the Middle East, and Africa that are run by strongmen or have political systems based on inherited titles, China's political noninterference is a welcome respite from American meddling. Despite what you read in *The New York Times* and other US media outlets, China enjoys generally warm relations with most other countries in Asia. Former Malaysian prime minister Mahathir Mohamad has urged ASEAN to move toward China after "US provocations" over Taiwan.[5] Anwar Ibrahim said, after becoming

Malaysia's prime minister, that ties with China were "pivotal" and that he hoped to enhance ties with Beijing and that America should stop its "Chinaphobia."[6] Indonesia's President Prabowo Subianto declared that he "fully supports the development of closer Indonesia–China relations and wishes to continue President Joko's policy of friendship with China."[7] China enjoys similarly strong relations with other neighbors like Thailand and Laos, and even relations with Vietnam are warming.

Companies have to decide whether to incorporate Chinese or American technology—the US is strong-arming allies by making it clear that it won't let them use Chinese technology. If they do, the US has warned countries like Germany that it won't share military intelligence as freely with them.

Biden's sanctions are bringing pain both to Chinese businesses that no longer have access to the best technology and so sell inferior-end products and to American technology firms that see their potential Chinese client base shrinking. Companies at the end of the value chain are being forced to utilize substandard products at higher prices causing higher prices for end consumers. For example, because America banned Huawei telecom equipment under the Secure Equipment Act of 2021, it is estimated American telecom companies will have to waste 5.6 billion US dollars ripping Huawei and ZTE equipment out of their telecom systems. American customers also no longer can buy Huawei phones which often sell for 30 percent less than Apple equivalents with similar specifications.[8]

In the short term, Chinese firms will suffer from the sanctions as they do not have access to the top technology and they have fewer potential customers to target. But in the long term, the sanctions will strengthen China's technology sector and make it more innovative and competitive. China's success with its space program is a prime example of how China will innovate in order to overcome American sanctions. The Wolf Amendment passed in 2011 banned the National Aeronautics and Space Administration (NASA) from cooperating with China. NASA banned China from visiting and cooperating on the International Space Station (ISS). Instead of ending its ambitions to explore space, America forced China to build its own space station, the Tiangong space station. Its first module, the *Tianhe*, was launched in 2021 and is one-fifth the size of the ISS. No matter how many barriers the US puts in front of China, China will simply continue to innovate and focus on indigenous innovation and not allow its technological ambitions to be thwarted. It is myopic of America to think that China will roll over in the face of sanctions and not innovate.

China will continue to focus on indigenous innovation—in everything from semiconductors to NEVs, to cloud computing and artificial intelligence—to reduce its national security risk and to find new growth drivers for its economy. Sanctions combined with ambitious and well-financed Chinese start-ups mean fewer opportunities for Western businesses to play an active role in selling into the high end of the technology supply chain in China. Foreign brands may focus sales efforts on private Chinese firms, but the reality is that Chinese firms will buy Chinese-made products whenever they can to ensure a steady supply chain. American and European companies in the tech sector are better off reallocating sales resources to grow outside China. They should focus efforts on selling to the G7 nations, home markets, and to countries in the Global South that are close to America politically like India.

Sanctions will force Chinese technology companies to focus on indigenous innovation in a do-or-die situation and provide opportunities for investors that back them.

Eventually, Chinese players will produce good enough technology or even technology better than American players and grab market share by selling both to China and the Global South. Investors should invest in the sectors the government is pushing to become new growth drivers like semiconductors and NEVs and back national champions that are innovating and taking global market share.

Notes

1. Billy House and Francine Lacqua, Interview with Nancy Pelosi, *Bloomberg.com*, last updated September 1, 2023, https://www.bloomberg.com/news/articles/2023-08-31/pelosi-says-chinese-leaders-lack-shared-values-with-us

2. James Mackintosh, "Lessons from a Three-Decade-Long Stock Market Disaster," *Wall Street Journal*, February 22, 2024, https://www.wsj.com/finance/stocks/lessons-from-a-three-decade-long-stock-market-disaster-5a0b5435

3. K. W., "Toshiba Yesterday, Huawei Today!" *Investor*, February 13, 2019, https://klse.i3investor.com/web/blog/detail/kianweiaritcles/2019-02-13-story-h1457038307-Toshiba_yesterday_Huawei_today

4. Peng Heyue, "China's Indigenous Innovation Policy and Its Effect on Foreign Intellectual Property Rights Holders," *King and Wood China Law Insight*, September 9, 2010, https://www.chinalawinsight.com/2010/09/articles/intellectual-property/chinas-indigenous-innovation-policy-and-its-effect-on-foreign-intellectual-property-rights-holders/

5. Mercedes Ruehl and Oliver Telling, "Mahathir Mohamad Urges ASEAN to Move Towards China after US's Taiwan 'Provocation,'" August 29, 2022, https://www.ft.com/content/0f80bc63-7e07-4396-a496-2c125c597014

6. *Financial Times* interview with Anwar Ibrahim quoted in "Malaysia's Prime Minister Doesn't Want to Choose Between the

U.S. and China: 'Why Must I be Tied to One Interest,'" *Fortune*, February 26, 2024, https://fortune.com/asia/2024/02/26/malaysia-prime-minister-anwar-ibrahim-does-not-want-to-choose-between-china-us/

7. "Prabowo Promises Close Ties with China in Meeting with Xi," *Jakarta Post*, April 2, 2024, https://www.thejakartapost.com/world/2024/04/02/prabowo-promises-close-ties-with-china-in-meeting-with-xi.html

8. Igor Bonifacic, "US Carriers Ask the FCC for $5.6 Billion to Replace Huawei and ZTE Equipment," *Engadget*, February 6, 2022, https://www.engadget.com/fcc-huawei-zte-rip-replace-funding-211116669.html

CHAPTER 5

Commodities

Agricultural Self-Reliance and De-dollarization

Under cover of darkness on September 26, 2022, state-sponsored terrorists blew up Russia's Nord Stream underwater pipeline to Europe, spewing liquefied natural gas (LGN) into the Baltic Sea. Who was behind the destruction? No one has claimed responsibility but allegations abound. Was it Putin's Russia? Was it America? Was it Norway or another NATO-aligned country? Regardless of who was behind the sabotage, the destruction left two things clear—first, Russia no longer has energy leverage over Europe and, second, Europe would go cold without Russian LNG or have to pay higher prices to get LNG from other countries like America.

The crown jewel of Putin's energy empire, the Nord Stream pumped Russian LNG to heat European homes at a fraction of previous prices. Forty percent of European gas needs flowed through Nord Stream, enriching Russia and allowing Moscow to maintain its influence despite the break-up of the Soviet empire.[1] While China has its near monopoly in rare earths for leverage and America its semiconductors, Russia had the LNG pipeline.

For proponents of free markets, the pipeline symbolized how cooperation between Russia and Germany in the post–World War II era could forge economic interdependence. For economic globalists like former German chancellor Gerhard Schröder, energy cooperation between the two countries reduced the risk of war. Russia and Germany had to cooperate or they would go cold or broke.

Not everyone supported Europe's reliance on Russia for its energy needs even before Russia's invasion of Ukraine. Poland's erstwhile minister of defense (now minister of foreign affairs) Radosław Sikorski compared the agreement to the infamous Nazi-era Molotov–Ribbentrop Pact in the lead-up to World War II. Sikorksi warned Russia could never be trusted because of a cultural predilection for war. The pipeline left Europe dependent on Russia and unable to secure national security interests.

Until Russia's invasion of Ukraine, globalists and economic interdependence advocates held sway. But as the shelling killed innocent civilians, criticism of Europe's dependence on Russia for its energy needs rose. How could Europe arm Ukraine yet at the same time be beholden to Russia for its energy needs?

Once the pipeline was destroyed, Europe no longer depended on Russia but suffered from high LNG prices. Inflation struck Europe, leaving many European families to choose between eating and keeping warm during the harsh 2022–23 winter. Exports from China to Europe for electric blankets and space heaters soared. Only China had the manufacturing and logistics capacities to ramp up electric blanket production to get product to Europe in time, underscoring the fact that it won't lose its position as the world's factory.

The lack of natural gas and the harsh winter made Europe realize it could never be beholden again to Russia or any other non-European country. Calls for de-risking from China by German politicians, especially China hawks in the Green

Party like Foreign Minister Annalena Baerbock and Reinhard Bütikofer, rose to a crescendo.

Biden claimed the attack on Nord Stream was a "deliberate act of sabotage." He did not claim Putin was behind the sabotage but accused Putin of "pumping out disinformation and lies" about who had blown up the pipeline.[2] Biden never explained why Russia would want to blow up its main instrument of leverage over Europe and lose the hard currency selling LNG brought.

Putin claimed it was the "Anglo-Saxons" and hinted in an interview with the conservative commentator and talk show host Tucker Carlson that it was the CIA that blew the pipeline up to limit Russia's power and to create opportunities for America to profit by selling American LNG to Europe.[3]

China agreed with Putin's conclusions that America was behind the attack. Why would Russia blow up its own pipeline? Without the Nord Stream, Russia could not fill its coffers with foreign currency and Putin lost its leverage over Europe. Russia blowing up its own pipeline would be like China blowing up rare-earth refineries—it just did not make sense.

On the other hand, the US gained from the sabotage. American secretary of state Antony Blinken touted the destruction as a "great opportunity" for America to sell more LNG to Europe. America took advantage of the situation and sold LNG to Europe for quadruple the price in the US. Even though shipping added to the costs, Europeans were outraged at the high prices.

France's President Macron and finance minister Bruno Le Maire took umbrage at the high prices and complained that America was taking advantage of its European allies to profit. Macron's anger led him to visit China where he declared Europe cannot be a tool of America. To drive a wedge between

France and the US, during the visit China showered Macron with praise and bought 160 Airbus planes.

China's leaders were not surprised by American actions to profit from Europe's energy problems. Chinese believe the US makes allegations against other nations about human rights abuses or aggression in order to justify containing countries with large natural resource reserves so the US can sell their own natural resources or commandeer them. They believe America labels countries with energy reserves like Iran or Venezuela who refuse to be vassal states as committing human rights abuses while hypocritically turning a blind eye to human rights abuses in countries like Israel that are American allies.

At the onset of Russia's invasion of Ukraine, China predicted the US would not seek immediate peace via diplomatic means—they expected the US to prolong the war in order to weaken Putin in a proxy war, try to force the Russian people to overthrow Putin, and as a means to warn China not to engage in military aggression against Taiwan. Moreover, the longer the war went on, Chinese analysts surmised, the US could profit more from selling more LNG and weapons.

Controlling commodities for power

America uses its influence over commodity supply chains in seeds and cotton as a means of exerting power over the Global South. In his book *Super Imperialism*, Michael Hudson argues the US forces African nations to use the US dollar to buy its seeds to grow crops like cocoa. By forcing African nations to use the US dollar for transactions and by basing the crop growing on American seeds, the US wields power over Africa. If African nations refused to follow American foreign policy, the US, Hudson contended, could starve Africa by not sending seeds. Hudson called the World Bank and the IMF the most "evil" organizations in the world for the power they wield over Africa.[4]

Control over commodities and pricing them in US dollars has long been critical to making the US dollar the world's reserve currency. Countries are moving away from holding the US dollar as a reserve currency due the US weaponization of SWIFT against Russia and the confiscation of Russian oligarchs' assets without trial.[5] They are worried they, too, will one day have their assets confiscated by US actions that have created unintended consequences that will hurt American financial dominance in the long term.

Businessmen from countries like Saudi Arabia and China worry they might be next on the sanctions list, so like China's Central Bank they have reduced their US dollar holdings and moved assets out of the UK and America to countries like Singapore that better protect the rights of account holders and reduces the reliance on SWIFT. Chinese officials have also focused on building China's own sources of commodities, from agricultural products like rice to energy supplies, to ensure national security.

Like Europeans and Americans who want to de-risk from China and Russia, forces within China want to de-risk from America and Europe. China is pushing self-reliance in food supplies. If China can't produce something itself, it will buy from friendly nations like Brazil while reducing purchases from America. There are huge opportunities for investment in China in the commodity sector, especially agricultural, as China seeks self-reliance in food supplies.

After the weaponization of SWIFT, countries within the Global South are also pushing for de-dollarization and a search for a new reserve currency—they fear that they, too, will be sanctioned if they ever cross DC. Brazilian president Luiz Inácio Lula da Silva has said there should be a BRICS currency, and others have pushed for the adoption of China's yuan, even though it is not yet freely convertible. China itself reduced its US dollar holdings to a 14-year low by October 2023 to 769.6 billion USD and Chinese have been buying more gold.[6] Russia and India are considering trading in the United Arab Emirates' dirham, and many countries are buying bonds priced in yuan. The yuan will be the long-term big winner of the shift away from the US dollar as a reserve currency—China's noninterventionist policies in other countries' affairs make other countries less worried about being sanctioned by China.

China's worries that America wants to contain its renewable energy and commodity sectors like cotton and other agricultural products. Over the last 20 years, China has emerged as a major producer of cotton, accounting for 24 percent of the world total, and has taken the lead in solar panel innovation.[7] Almost all of China's cotton and solar panels are manufactured in China's Xinjiang Province, the province the Biden regime not coincidentally claims that genocide and forced labor are taking place.

Few ethnically Han Chinese believe China commits genocide against China's Uyghurs and balk at the US allegations. Ben Lowsen, a columnist for *The Diplomat*, and a China advisor to the US Air Force, claims China has enslaved tens of millions of Uyghurs. The allegations have become a cause célèbre in the Western world, with former US secretary of state Mike Pompeo and former NBA player Enes Kanter claiming China commits genocide against Uyghurs despite their population increasing by 16 percent between 2010 and 2020 to 11.6 million.[8]

Rebutting the allegations, China's government claims accusations of genocide and slave labor are unfounded. China claims it preserves and respects Uyghur culture by teaching the Uyghur language in classrooms but also by teaching Mandarin to equip Uyghur youth with the tools necessary to find good careers throughout the country. Teaching Mandarin has been called "cultural genocide" by critics in America.

Everyday Chinese have gotten angry at what they consider to be unfounded allegations. The result is that Chinese have boycotted buying Nike, H&M, adidas, and other foreign sports apparel brands that refuse to source cotton from Xinjiang. Chinese buy sports apparel from Chinese brands like Li Ning and Anta that promise to keep buying Xinjiang cotton. Chinese consumers believe America makes allegations in order to stop the growth of China's cotton and solar panel industries and therefore have become more patriotic in their purchases.

A firsthand visit to Xinjiang

I decided to visit Xinjiang to see firsthand the cotton fields and factories. I wanted to see whether or not there was credibility to America's allegations. As someone who lost family on my father's side to the Holocaust, I am sensitive to allegations of genocide. If I saw genocide or forced labor, I promised myself I would not keep my mouth shut even if that hurt my business interests.

I visited Xinjiang three times in 2021 and 2022, spending almost one month there. On two visits, I traveled with Chinese state media giant Xinhua News which paid my way. During the day, I traveled with Xinhua but, although I was part of a curated tour and had minders from the Ministry of Publicity, formerly called the Ministry of Propaganda, was able to stop the caravan wherever I wanted and was free to ask whatever questions I had. At night, I could go out by myself, without anyone knowing where I was and with whom I talked—for example, one night at midnight I played basketball with Uyghur teenagers in Aksu City.

On my third visit in 2022, I paid my own way and traveled with my son. I traveled freely and asked any questions I wanted, although one government official called me in once to have tea to discuss what I was doing. I told her I was following Chinese law and could go anywhere I wanted and ask whatever questions I wanted. After our meeting, no government official interfered with my movements and questions.

The one major difference in the answers I got when I traveled with Xinhua and when I went alone was that, in the latter case, respondents admitted to there being serious ethnic tension between Han Chinese and Uyghurs. However, in my interviews, the vast majority of Uyghurs said tension existed but the situation had gotten much better since 2018. Over 90 percent who complained of racial tension said the central government played a positive role in mitigating animosity. Much of the discontent was based on what may seem to be relatively small things like pork—most Uyghurs are Muslim and do not eat pork while pork is the main protein for many Han Chinese.

Uyghurs and other Muslim minorities like the Hui did complain at times of too much heavy-handedness in the implementation of policies. For example, I met one 18-year-old girl in Kashgar. She initially wanted to take us to visit her home village but canceled because she said it was too troublesome—she had to report to local authorities whenever any visitor came to her home from outside her village and she did not want to go through all the hassle. She did not view the requirement as malign but annoying and cumbersome.

Another 31-year-old practicing Muslim told me the police would check him at his hotel at midnight when he traveled outside of Xinjiang which was dehumanizing. He said the police were always polite but that it was not fair that he had to be checked. He also said it was wrong his father was forced to attend classes for three months where he learned Mandarin and was forced to listen to CPC propaganda. He was angry because his father could not earn money during the three months. The father was allowed to return home every night. But, in the end, this Muslim supported the CPC because they made Xinjiang "safe" and no one had hurt his father. Even if he did not agree with policies that infringed on his family's life, he said the policies did not derive from an ill-intentioned place.

Not one Uyghur claimed to me to have heard of genocide, even those Uyghurs who hated the Chinese government. One woman in Urumqi told me "the government does bad things" but never claimed genocide. Other Uyghurs told me they did not like the Chinese government because it was heavy-handed and limited personal freedoms, but even they did not support claims of genocide.

Visiting a Xinjiang cotton field

I was standing in a sweeping cotton field that seemed endless, talking to a sixty-something-year-old Uyghur farmer. He smiled. "We have the best cotton in the world. No cotton, not even in the United States, is fluffier than our cotton in Xinjiang."

The farmer bent over and picked up a cotton ball from a shrub and placed it in my hands. "Feel," he said, while rolling the cotton between his fingers. "The best in the world!" He put his arm around my shoulder and pointed to fields of white fluffy cotton and beamed. "No one makes better cotton than we do here in Xinjiang. No one."

I was in Aksu meeting with cotton farmers, cotton field workers, and factory owners along with reporters from Xinhua News. This is where America claimed genocide and forced labor were taking place.

The old man owned his cotton fields and picked the cotton himself along with his wife and a few workers. As we sat in the outdoor courtyard of his home, he cracked a walnut open with his bare hands and said, "Twenty years ago, I paid workers only two or three yuan a day to pick cotton. Now, it costs me 300 a day. I can't even find workers from Xinjiang to pick cotton anymore, because it is too difficult a job, and there too many good job opportunities in Xinjiang. I have to recruit from Gansu Province if I need any workers. Frankly, however, rising labor costs are not my biggest problem."

He sighed. "My biggest problem is that American economic sanctions prevent me from buying American cotton-picking equipment. Even though Chinese manufacturing has gotten better, America still makes the best cotton-picking equipment. Right now, 95 percent of the cotton-picking process is automated."

American cotton-picking equipment companies like John Deere made a fortune selling into Xinjiang before sanctions blocked them. In the quarter before American implemented sanctions, John Deere's sales increased over 4000 percent as Xinjiang cotton field farm owners bought American equipment before sanctions kicked in.[9]

The farmer discussed his challenges because of sanctions: "Aside from not being able to buy equipment, I can't export overseas. We will be fine as China is a large enough market on its own." If Biden was trying to help Uyghurs in Xinjiang, his plan seem to be backfiring as Uyghurs lose sales opportunities, I thought to myself.

Sanctions on Xinjiang illustrate how America impoverishes the very people, like the Uyghur cotton farmer, they are supposedly trying to help. For the farmer, he could deduce no other reason for the sanctions than a simple money grab by America. He told me: "The US was trying to contain China's cotton growth unfairly because it did not want to lose its dominant position."

Not only do the sanctions hurt Uyghurs and Han Chinese but they hurt American businesses, too. Like Intel and Google, which lost Huawei as a client, John Deere lost out on selling to Xinjiang cotton companies.

After visiting the small farm, Xinhua took me to tour a conglomerate run mostly by Han Chinese executives. As I walked into the factory area, senior executives told me I could take pictures anywhere, talk to anyone I wanted, and visit any part of the factory. They only placed one limit—they did not want me to take photos that mentioned their company name. They worried American eyes would see how big they had become and slap sanctions on them. They believed any company in Xinjiang would be targeted for sanctions once they reached a certain scale.

"Who owns all of the cotton fields?" I asked an executive of the company, a Han Chinese born in Xinjiang. He told me the company does not own the cotton fields directly. The company pays rent to the Uyghur owners, to pick the cotton and then process it to be sold. The factory also buys cotton directly from Uyghur farmers who harvest and process their cotton themselves.

The executive drove me to sprawling fields and explained the owners of the fields were Uyghurs who had combined their smaller plots of farmland to create a unified force to negotiate for better prices. The Uyghur families received a fixed rent and a share of revenues. A few farmers had decided not to join the collective, the executive explained to me and decided to harvest their crop themselves.

One thirty-something Uyghur owner who did not rent out his plot told me, "I can earn more by working the fields myself. But it is hard work." He had pride in managing his own plot and producing great cotton.

I heard a large ch-ch-ch-ch chopping sound, almost like a helicopter. I looked up and saw two Uyghurs laughing as they piloted a DJI drone. They used the drone to drop pesticide on the cotton plants. I asked how much the drone had cost them. They told me that drones cost 20,000 USD but were faster and cheaper than using human labor.

Most Han Chinese I have interviewed outside of Xinjiang are skeptical of America's claims of genocide and forced labor. They see Uyghurs walking around China on a daily basis. Xinjiang restaurants can be found throughout the country owned and/or staffed by Uyghurs. The Chinese government is actively promoting tourism to Xinjiang by Han Chinese and using Uyghur models with advertisements promoting the respect of Uyghur traditional culture. Many of China's most famous celebrities come from Xinjiang like the actress and singer Dilraba Dilmurat and have publicly voiced support for the government. Dilraba Dilmurat used to endorse sports-apparel maker adidas but dropped them in protest after adidas said it would stop buying Xinjiang cotton.[10]

Despite not finding evidence of genocide or forced labor, I did find policies that could be criticized as heavy-handed and open to legitimate criticism. For example, Muslims cannot go to a mosque until the age of 18. After the age of 18, they are free to practice their religion. Limiting younger people from attending mosque, however, is not a targeted policy against Muslims or Uyghurs. No one in China with Chinese citizenship—including Christians, Jews, Buddhists, Muslims, and Taoists—are allowed to go to places of worship and officially practice religion until the age of 18. Whenever I go to a Passover service in China, I have to show proof of foreign citizenship.

I can understand why some criticize policies limiting children from attending religious services if parents want their children to be raised in their faith. However, limiting access to mosques to adults is not genocide or even cultural genocide—it is an attempt to ensure religious-led protests and revolutions like the Taiping Rebellion (1850–64) do not happen again. Today's China is as wary of how religion can cause social instability as it has been throughout its history.

Making citizens report visitors to local authorities like that 18-year-old would have to do if she took me to her village is arguably also overkill and might be considered repressive. For a time, too, Han officials lived with local Uyghur families in a campaign to promote understanding. That initiative received criticism from Uyghurs and Hans alike who objected to the policy so the government ended the campaign.

Mandarin has also become the main language taught in schools in Xinjiang. But as one Uyghur teacher in Kashgar told me, "We teach our kids Mandarin, Uyghur and English!" Parents I interviewed welcome Mandarin training in schools to equip their children with the language skills necessary to find good jobs. Most Chinese view China's language policies in schools to be similar to that of teaching English in American schools. A country needs an official language.

False allegations of human rights abuses?

There is a widespread belief in China that America makes up allegations about genocide to justify sanctions on fast-growing sectors like cotton and solar panels to try to contain the country, just as it did Japan. Chinese consumers have reacted with a mix of anger and patriotism to what they see as containment policies.

Anger against America has led many Chinese to buy domestic Chinese brands in a trend called *guocha*. To tout their Chinese identity, firms like sports apparel companies like Anta and Li Ning have pledged to buy Xinjiang cotton. Chinese, however, have bought more sneakers from American brand Skechers to support it because it has said that it has not found evidence of forced labor in Xinjiang. Overall, more Chinese consumers buy handset makers like Honor or Xiaomi and home appliances from Midea and Gree in a show of patriotism.

The shift toward buying domestic brands is nothing new but it has been accelerated by the attacks on Xinjiang's cotton and a feeling that America and her allies are bullying China. In 2011, my company, the China Market Research Group (CMR), interviewed 5000 consumers in 15 cities across China. Eighty-five percent of respondents said they would always buy a foreign brand over a local brand. At the time, foreign brands provided more brand cachet and prestige to their buyers, giving them face and they trusted that they had purchased a good-quality product. There were many fears at the time that Chinese products were cheap, bad quality, or even toxic. Many domestic Chinese companies cut corners in search of profits, using bad-quality glue in furniture making, poor-quality dyes in clothes, and even melamine in dairy products.

By 2016, my firm started to see a shift. We replicated the research and found 60 percent of Chinese consumers said they would buy a domestic Chinese brand over a foreign brand. Savvy Chinese companies, often backed by foreign private equity firms, realized offering good-quality products equated to more profits in the long term. By 2021, research showed 85 percent of consumers preferred to purchase domestic Chinese brands over foreign brands. Chinese were proud of their country and angry at what they perceived as attempts to contain China's rise.

Despite the *guochao* trend, China still holds great opportunities for foreign brands. But the days of easy sales are gone as domestic rivals now vie on quality, innovation, and price. Foreign brands need to understand the fast-changing Chinese consumer and launch new product lines with fast production and sales cycles. They need to launch marketing and messaging specific to China. Translating ad campaigns or even products created in Europe or the US into Chinese will no longer suffice. Brands need to create sleeve lengths, for example, that fit Chinese body types. They can't simply sell the same-sized clothes in Shanghai that they sell in London—body shapes are different.

Right now, the only foreign brands with economic moats (as compared to domestic Chinese brands) would be in sectors with strong brand heritage like sports cars, cosmetics, and luxury goods. Even then, these moats are getting smaller. Previously, Chinese wanted to buy Samsung or Apple mobile handsets over Chinese ones. Chinese consumers now view mobile phones as commodities, which is why Xiaomi, Oppo, and Vivo have seized market share

The automotive industry was one of the last sectors to attract Chinese consumers to Chinese brands, but the shift toward NEVs has shown that even the automotive sector has become commoditized. The technology of domestic players like Li Xiang and BYD are comparable to Tesla and are perceived by some consumers to be better than legacy auto makers like Volkswagen and Nissan. Even Porsche has started to struggle, as one senior executive admitted to me, because

"We are not necessarily better in NEVs than Chinese counterparts and our cars are too expensive right now compared with Li Xiang and NIO."

The only sector whose moat is still intact, then, are the luxury brands, where, no matter how good the marketing and products are, it is impossible for Chinese firms to replicate the heritage underlying brands like Hermès and Chanel.

Profiting from new commodity supply chains

Fear over sanctions like those that hit Russia is forcing the Chinese government to look to secure new commodity supply chains and to focus on self-sufficiency in food security. Instead of relying on Australia or America for beef for example, China is diversifying its supply chain to buy beef from friendlier nations like Brazil and Uruguay. Countries and businesses in the Global South can gain profits by selling commodities to China. Businesses that can export fruit like mangoes, avocado, and durian or seafoods like lobster that cannot easily be farmed in China, will have huge market potential.

However, most importantly, China has been beefing up—pun tended—its own cattle-rearing abilities, as well as the domestic food supply chain. After India banned the export of many forms of popular rice, China doubled down on its efforts for more self-sufficiency in staple crops like rice. Foreign and Chinese business should begin to cultivate fields in China for foods, from coffee beans to blueberries to kiwis. The government is actively supporting the growth of the domestic food supply chain to ensure national security. For example, Alibaba founder Jack Ma, whom we will learn about in the next chapter, has shifted his focus from tech to focus on agriculture.

The bombing of Nord Stream has caused a chain of un-intended consequences in the global economy—China will focus on bolstering local agricultural and commodity supply chains, Chinese consumers are becoming more patriotic in their purchase decisions, and the Global South is pushing for de-dollarization. The end result is a weakening of American power. The Global South is wary of US hegemony after America's weaponization of SWIFT, confiscation of Russian assets, and allegations backed by no evidence of China's committing genocide and forced labor in Xinjiang. China influence will continue to rise in the Global South and create a shift toward a multipolar world.

Notes

1. David McHugh, "Explainer: What's Russia's Nord Stream 2 Pipeline to Europe?" *Associated Press*, February 8, 2022, https://apnews.com/article/russia-ukraine-nord-stream-2-oil-pipeline-779970ee17f6fa9d0fa2996e45cbeab9

2. Allie Malloy and Maegan Vazquez, "Biden Calls Nord Stream Pipelines Leaks a 'Deliberate Act of Sabotage,'" *CNN*, September 30, 2022, https://www.cnn.com/2022/09/30/politics/biden-ukraine-putin-pipeline/index.html#:~:text=President%20Joe%20Biden%20on%20Friday,accuse%20Moscow%20for%20the%20leaksweaponiz

3. Tucker Carlson, Interview with Vladimir Putin, *The Tucker Carlson Interview*, The Tucker Carlson Network, February 9, 2024, https://youtu.be/hYfByTcY49k?si=6hghqso0CS1GmnEQ

4. Michael Hudson, *Super Imperialism*, 2nd edn. (London: Pluto Press, 2003); Michael Hudson, "The Hard Fist of American Imperialism," *Michael Hudson on Finance, Real Estate, and the Powers of Neoliberalism*, April 26, 2020, https://michael-hudson.com/2020/04/the-hard-fist-of-american-imperialism/

5. Created in 1973, SWIFT is the finance system that links 11,000 banks and institutions to allow the rapid transfer of money across country borders. Russian banks were banned from using SWIFT, meaning that Russia cannot use foreign currency easily to make and receive payments for sales, for example, of its LNG. Russell Hotten, "Ukraine Conflict: What is Swift and Why is Banning Russia So Significant," *BBC News*, May 4, 2022, https://www.bbc.com/news/business-60521822

6. "China Continues to Reduce Its Holdings of US Treasuries in October," *Global Times*, December 20, 2023, https://www.globaltimes.cn/page/202312/1303982.shtml#:~:text=China's%20overall%20holdings%20of%20US,of%20%2497.5%20billion%20within%202023

7. Chuck Abbott, "After Reaching 'Peak Cotton,' a Declining Role for China," *Successful Farming*, August 10, 2022, https://www.agriculture.com/news/business/after-reaching-peak-cotton-a-declining-role-for-china

8. Yi Fuxian, "Why is the Uyghur Population Shrinking," *Project Syndicate*, July 12, 2022, https://www.project-syndicate.org/commentary/Xinjiang-Uyghur-crackdown-population-decline-by-yi-fuxian-2022-07?barrier=accesspaylog#:~:text=The%20data%20show%20that%20in,of%20that%20aged%205%2D9

9. Jacob Fromer, Cissy Zhou, and Finbarr Bermingham, "US Farm Brand John Deere at Forefront of Surging Cotton Machinery Sales to Xinjiang, as Human Rights Sanctions Loom," *South China Morning Post*, August 8, 2020, https://www.scmp.com/economy/china-economy/article/3096510/us-farm-brand-john-deere-forefront-surging-cotton-machinery

10. Julia Yeo, "Eason Chan, Dilireba & Other Chinese Celebs Boycott Nike & Adidas to Stand with Xinjiang Cotton," *Mothership*, April 1, 2021, https://mothership.sg/2021/04/chinese-hk-celebs-nike-adidas-xinjiang/

CHAPTER 6

The Tech Crackdown

Hitting Alibaba and Tencent

"China is un-investable right now," groused Joe, a billion-aire hedge fund founder. "The crackdown on tech firms like Alibaba has left so much uncertainty for investors and is just plain wrong. Why would the government destroy Alibaba?"

I was talking with one of the world's wealthiest men and long one of the world's biggest China bulls. Originally, Joe had made his money investing in the stock market and had made billions investing in Alibaba and Bitcoin.

All Chinese use Alibaba apps daily, whether it be for buying shoes, booking the latest blockbuster movie, purchasing health insurance and medicine, or trading stocks as part of a retirement portfolio. During Covid, Chinese citizens had to use either Alibaba's Alipay or Tencent's WeChat to scan health codes whenever they entered a building to prove they had had a recent Covid test. Joe benefited from Alibaba's dominance across so many sectors of China's economy.

Joe salivated at the IPO of Ant Financial, a subsidiary of Alibaba, much as investors had anticipated Facebook's IPO. Wall Street analysts estimated the IPO to be worth over 313 billion USD.[1] The size and scope of Ant Financial's business lines at the time would be like having Citigroup, AIG,

Blue Cross, Fidelity, Visa, and Walmart all wrapped into one company. Investors had never seen anything so big before.

Investing in Alibaba and Ant Financial's IPO was as close to a sure bet ... until it wasn't. One October morning in 2020, at the Bund Financial Summit in Shanghai, Alibaba's founder, Jack Ma, shook the investment and tech worlds by criticizing China's regulators. Ma called regulators old-fashioned and accused them of having a "pawnshop mentality."[2]

Before that day, Ma seemed to have the uncanny ability to get rich while placating the CPC echelons and navigating the minefields set by jealous state-owned enterprises. Bemused investors around the world telephoned me: Did Ma go crazy? Did he become too full of himself and think he was above Party oversight? Was this a last-ditch effort to fend off an impending crackdown?

Within days, regulators squashed Ant Financial's IPO and began the dismantling of Alibaba. What had looked set to be one of the world's largest ever IPOs hit a wall. One of Ant's potential investors, Fidelity, marked down Ant's valuation to just 70 billion USD.[3] Once a mainstay of television shows and thought leader events, Ma disappeared from public view aside from a few sightings of him in Hainan, Tokyo, and Spain, on vacation or scouting for investments.

Until the crackdown, Ma had taken on legendary status by appearing in martial arts clips and singing at Alibaba's annual 11/11 shopping day extravaganzas. He nurtured a Warren Buffett-like persona dishing out life advice. Ma became like Steve Jobs, Tony Robbins, and Elon Musk all rolled into one, spinning yarns and doling out tips to a hungry nation wanting to know how to get rich.

After his takedown, pundits argued Ma had gotten too rich and high profile and that this had caused the Party to take aim at him and Ant Financial. In many ways, Jack Ma had become the face of China to the rest of the world, an unofficial foreign minister of sorts. He sat on panels with former US president Bill Clinton and Tesla founder Elon Musk where he charmed Western audiences with homespun tales about how many times he had applied and failed to gain admission to Harvard.

When Canadian prime minister Justin Trudeau visited China, he met with Xi and then made a beeline to Hangzhou to carouse with Ma, skipping meetings with senior government officials. Ma said he had "great chemistry" with Trudeau and predicted he would help create "a lot of jobs" in Canada,[4] even though relations between China and Canada had gone south after the arrest of Huawei's CFO, Meng Wanzhou, and China retaliated by detaining the "Two Michaels," Michael Spavor and Michael Kovrig. Ma's relations with Trudeau were at odds with Xi's, who does not respect Trudeau. Xi was so disgusted by Trudeau's behavior he lectured him at the 2022 G20 meeting in Bali for spilling confidential information to the press, as if he were a misbehaving schoolboy.

Ma had also headed to New York to meet with Trump when he became president-elect. Despite Trump's trade war against China, Ma suggested Trump be given a chance because "at least he's trying." To those who didn't know better, it seemed Ma was Xi's emissary, trying to improve US–China relations by acting as a middleman.

Others viewed Ma as trying to usurp power from Xi by forcing his hand to accept Ma's trade deals. To those who understand how things work in China, Ma was clearly playing with fire by taking such public stands at odds with Xi. He had outstayed his welcome in government circles and among SOE executives by trying to outshine them.

Ma's influence on China's business community suddenly ended that October. He lost control of his company, even though his money was never taken away. Regulators moved to investigate Ant Financial and Alibaba. They levied billion-dollar fines.

Spooked by the crackdown on such a high-profile entrepreneur, Western investors like Joe fled the Chinese equity markets and started to buy equities in America, Japan, and India. If Xi could target Ma, Western investors worried, who would they target next? Investors feared China's newly minted billionaires in the technology space would be investigated if they retained their power. They stopped buying Chinese tech stocks like Deyu's.

The founders of social media giant ByteDance and ecommerce site Pinduoduo, Zhang Yiming and Huang (Colin) Zheng, stepped down from their positions as CEOs, further cementing fears among Western investors that no tech entrepreneurs would be allowed to have power in Xi's China.

Hong Kong's equity markets became one of the worst performing in 2022 and 2023, losing 7 trillion USD of value. Many investors echoed Joe's sentiments that China was no longer investable.[5] Many China-focused hedge funds rebranded themselves as pan-Asian funds as LP interest in all things China plummeted. As one broker for a bulge bracket broker told me, "All my China-focused clients have started learning Japanese. I guess I will have to as well."

Interest in China as an investment destination plummeted to multi-decade lows. China-focused private equity firms raised 11.6 billion USD in the first half of 2023, down from 300 billion USD in 2016.[6] Direct investors like Ontario Teachers' Pension Fund shut down their entire direct investing teams focused on China.

Despite rumors that the crackdown on Ma was due to his gaining too much wealth and power, the underlying reasons for the tech crackdown are more nuanced. The crackdown benefits China's technology sector in the long term as smaller companies like Deyu's will be able to grow without being strangled by large players. They will have a fair chance to grow and become global players. For equity investors, rather than making China un-investable, the crackdown makes China more investable in the long term by creating the opportunity for little dragons to become big dragons.

The government had to crack down on tech dominance by Alibaba and other major players like Tencent because they dominated so many ecosystems that they had started to stifle innovation, fair competition, and consumer choice. There were no little dragons during the reign of Alibaba and Tencent—their control over the tech sector meant tech start-ups had to become subsidiaries or go out of business.

Alibaba had its fingers in so many sectors, it also posed a systemic financial risk if it failed. It also had an outsized control of China's economy.

Within this context, Ma's words that October morning shocked not just because he criticized China's financial regulators but also because he downplayed the systemic threat Alibaba and Ant Financial posed to the financial system. Ma revealed he possessed a low-level understanding of credit and financial risk.

Neither Alibaba nor Ant Financial have been nationalized— they have been broken up and forced to end predatory practices to create more competition. This has allowed little dragons like Pinduoduo, Douyin, and Xiao Hong Shu (Red) to become big dragons. The government placed the same regulatory oversight on Ant Financial as other banks such as keeping reserves to backstop investor investments and accounts. Ant had been acting like a broker and bank, yet did not keep cash on hand or adhere to the same risk standards as other financial institutions like the Bank of China.

Alibaba and other tech giants were simply being forced to allow for fair competition from other companies, much as the US antitrust lawsuit against Microsoft forced Microsoft to end its monopoly position in the PC market by not allowing users to uninstall Internet Explorer and use other programs like Netscape and Java. In fact, China has not destroyed Alibaba—it has asked it to work with SOEs and be a key player in building China's semiconductor sector. In other words, the crackdown has minimized financial sector risks, spurred the development of little dragons in the tech space, and given consumers and brands more choice.

The rise of China's quasi-monopolies

Unburdened by the lumbering bureaucracy of SOEs, savvy Chinese entrepreneurs flocked to China's tech sector at the turn of the millennium. Flush with optimism and a spillover of investment cash from the dot.com era, American private equity firms backed Chinese internet darlings founded in the late 1990s like Sina, Sohu, and Netease that went public in America. Their IPOs scored riches for American investors and their LPs—American pension plans and endowments.

Internet leaders married into prominent Chinese political families. The CEO of Sina, Mao Daolin, married President Hu Jintao's daughter, symbolizing the merging of money and political power that marked the Hu Jintao era and creating the rise of the wealthy 10 percent—the registered residents living in Tier 1 cities like Beijing, Guangzhou, Shenzhen, and Shanghai and the wealthiest 10 percent of the population in all regions. Internet entrepreneurs gave stakes to the sons and daughters of the founding families of the Chinese Communist Party in return for connections and protection. American private equity firms, from Sequoia to GGV to Kleiner Perkins Caufield & Byers, set up shop in China as they sought the next generation of tech leaders.

Early Silicon Valley investors found the next generation of tech giants with the launch of Alibaba and smaller tech players like Ctrip, Qunar, Youkou, and Tudou. GGV was an early backer of Alibaba, generating billions in profits for their LPs. Based on their success of investing in Alibaba, GGV raised billions of dollars in subsequent funds. Softbank's Masayoshi Son turned a 20 million USD investment in Alibaba into a 50 billion USD stake that gave rise to his Vision Fund. The rise of China's tech giants created billion-dollar profits not just for Chinese but also for American and Japanese investors and their LPs.

China's best and brightest who did not want to climb the government ladder or get into real estate flocked to China's burgeoning tech sector, as Deyu did. Graduates from leading universities like Tsinghua and Peking Universities skipped jobs at traditional firms like management consultancy McKinsey and investment bank Goldman Sachs to seek training and riches in China's tech sector at Baidu, Alibaba, and Tencent, collectively nicknamed BAT. They all wanted to be the next Jack Ma.

By the 2010s, Alibaba and Tencent had pulled away from the competition, leaving Baidu in the dust, and a dark side to their dominance emerged—they essentially became a duopoly, stifling competition and consumer choice. Entrepreneurs set up companies not to be innovative and establish a trading market in their shares but to sell to Alibaba or Tencent. If a start-up had a good idea, they would get an investment from Alibaba. A clone would get investment from Tencent. Whether it was ride sharing, food delivery, payment systems, insurance, online doctors, pharmaceuticals, logistic firms, retailing, groceries, or plane and train tickets, Alibaba and Tencent had their fingers in every sector, boxing out all other competition.

These two players dominated so many sectors and created closed systems that they hurt competition and consumer choice. Starting a company in the internet space without getting an investment by one of the two became impossible. They would not let companies into their online ecosystem unless you took their investment. Companies under Alibaba's umbrella would only take payments, for example, through Alipay while companies under Tencent's umbrella would only take payment from WeChat. If you were not part of either ecosystem, there would be no easy way to transact payments. It even extended as far as provincial governments—I drove in Alibaba's home province of Zhejiang and was forced to pay a toll either in cash or Alipay. When I asked whether I could pay with Tencent Pay, the money collector said with a laugh: "Zhejiang is Alibabaland."

Entrepreneurs gussied up their companies to look innovative so as to do a trade sale to Tencent or Alibaba, rather than truly being innovative. Every key emerging sector had three start-ups—one got investment from Alibaba, another from Tencent, and the third typically failed. Entrepreneurs were backed by venture capitalists who backed clones and pushed for quick trade sales to make a quick buck.

Alibaba and Tencent leveraged their dominance to get fat margins while squeezing profits for everyone else. Brands had to pay huge percentages of their revenue to use platforms they controlled. Couriers made a pittance and often were not given social security while the founders became billionaires. Consumers did not have a choice where to buy, as Alibaba forced brands to sell exclusive products on online shopping sites Tmall or Taobao. In sum, while they had transformed and revolutionized China's economy and earned billions in profits for investors like Joe, Alibaba and Tencent had started to be a drag on the economy.

Mafia-like tactics

"Alibaba is like the Mafia," Adam, a senior executive for one of the world's largest apparel makers told me. "We sell so much volume on Taobao and Tmall … it's wonderful. The problem is our margins are squeezed. We have to do whatever Alibaba wants."

"When they tell us to discount, we have to discount," he continued. "When we tried to sell on rival platforms like Jingdong, Alibaba did not allow us." Even worse," he said, "you've got to worry about being penalized by Alibaba if we do something they do not like. Our margins are being squeezed. We have a love–hate relationship with Alibaba."

A love–hate relationship between Alibaba and retail executives was common before the crackdown. On the one hand, brands generated massive volumes selling on Alibaba's platforms if they spent heavily on Alibaba promotions. On the other hand, Alibaba strong-armed retailers, forcing them to sell products only on their platforms, discount heavily, and participate in the Double 11 (11/11) and June 18 (6/18) shopping holidays. The volumes from the shopping extravaganzas were a blessing and a curse for retailers.

An executive from an apparel maker summed up the problems: "Eighty percent of our annual online revenue came during the 11/11 shopping period. It is a nightmare for us because we have to rent warehouses at inflated rates for just a few months a year. It would be a lot better for us if we could have more steady online sales throughout the year than have everything artificially sold because of Alibaba events. The result is we have tiny margins on online sale even though we sell a ton of products."

Retailers became beholden to Alibaba's demands and strong-arm tactics. They could not choose when to discount; they could not choose which platforms to sell on. If they did not listen to Alibaba, they were shut off from access to Alibaba's hundreds of millions of customers. Operating much like a monopoly, Alibaba increased its profits by squeezing partners' margins. For brands seeking to gain a beachhead into China's consumer market, adhering to Alibaba's conditions was worth the tradeoff at first. China-based executives would tell headquarters that the goal was market share and sales volume and that profits would come later. But after years of huge volumes with anemic profits, the headquarters of multinational corporations started to balk at their relationship with Alibaba.

Brands started to complain about the unequal relationship. The government took note of the coercive elements in Alibaba's playbook. As part of China's Common Prosperity drive, they cracked down on Alibaba and other internet players like Meituan that stifled fair competition and created profits for the 10 percent on the backs of the 90 percent.

Rising income inequality

Under Xi Jinping, the CPC has made a strong turn to socialism where the emphasis is on creating a more egalitarian society and a large middle class. Marxism formed the foundation of the political thinking of the Deng Xiaoping, Jiang Zemin, and Hu Jintao eras but had often been a secondary consideration in the pragmatic drive to create jobs.

Almost a billion people were pulled out of poverty in the three decades after China's 1978 economic reforms. In 2021,

Xi declared China had eradicated extreme poverty in the previous decade by lifting the remaining 100 million out of it.

For all of its economic success since the reform movement, China faced a new challenge: the Gini coefficient got wider and wider as the rich like Jack Ma and the 10 percent earned earth-shaking sums. In the 1960s and 1970s, the difference between the poor and rich in China might have been having access to meat or clothes, with only a few government officials having access to private cars. By the 2010s, however, some of the 10 percent could afford private jets and multiple hundred-million-dollar homes around the world. The widening gap between the 10 percent and the 90 percent started to cause social turbulence and calls for a fairer society. Xi and the CPC have moved to recommit to the importance of a Marxist society that accepts private business but also pushes for more income equality and more equitable opportunities.

Chinese society was becoming unfair, with the 10 percent controlling too much of the economy while the 90 percent struggled. Political theorists like Wang Huning gained in power and influence under Xi. Once dean of the law school at Fudan University and advisor to Presidents Jiang Zemin and Hu Jintao, Wang became the fourth highest-ranking member of the CPC. He has long been a proponent of ushering in an era of socialism and has been critical of the American economic system where the rich like Citadel's Kenneth C. Griffin or George Soros donate legally to super political actional committees (super PACS) to help politicians get elected—arguably a form of legalized corruption.

Internet billionaires making money off the backs of the masses is no longer acceptable during Xi's reign. Restaurant owners told me that restaurant platform services like Ele. me and Meituan are a mixed blessing, much as retailers said about Alibaba. Restaurants used platforms to drive sales but profits were illusory as they had to pay too much to the platforms.

Old Wang, the owner of a small chain of Japanese restaurants in Shanghai, told me, "I don't make a lot of money selling through Meituan. I get huge volumes." For the consumer, it's convenient to order on Meituan. The problem is, Old Wang continued, Meituan takes a huge percentage of the overall ticket price with a commission between 16 and 26 percent so his profit margins are dead. If people come and eat at his restaurant, he makes money. If they order through online delivery which became more popular during Covid, he does not make much money.[7]

As with Alibaba and retailers, Meituan dominated the food delivery space. Meituan strong-armed restaurants into giving up huge cuts of their revenue. As consumers increasingly dined at home, especially during the Covid era, many restaurants went out of business if they did not have a home delivery option. At the same time, their profits were almost wholly being given to giant internet players because it was too costly and expensive for them to set up their own courier systems. The government found this was not fair and stepped in to ensure restaurants got a fair cut of sales from the internet players.

Couriers for Meituan, too, did not make much, which the government has moved to rectify. Meituan did not offer health care coverage to couriers and gave them tight deadlines to deliver food or face stiff fines and penalties. Couriers rode motorbikes on sidewalks and careered through office buildings, endangering others in their quest to deliver food on time and to get higher commissions. The founder of Meituan, Wang Xing, became a billionaire but the couriers who deliver goods for his company made only 10,000 RMB (under 1,400 USD) a month working 15 hours a day. Part of the crackdown forced Meituan to create better working conditions for couriers, all part of the ideological underpinning of Xi's interpretation of a Marxist society.

The tech crackdown should therefore not be viewed purely as an attack on business or the 10 percent, even though a consequence of the new policies hampers the ability for tech entrepreneurs to get rich and stifles their "animal spirits"—the human emotions that awaken the human mind and get people excited and optimistic to invest.

It is true sometimes the CPC has an uneasy relationship with private enterprise—the CPC understands the need for the private sector for job creation, but it wants to make sure no single company dominates entire ecosystems and thereby stifles innovation and competition.

The CPC also has a predilection for trying to control every aspect of the economy and society and does not like private enterprises that get so powerful they begin to unduly influence policymaking. The CPC also does not want the rich to make too much money by taking advantage of the poor. In the coming decade, Xi and the CPC will focus on building up the size and vibrancy of the middle class—the 90 percent—by squeezing the margins of businesses run by the 10 percent.

Officials need to make sure crackdowns do not go too far and kill the animal spirits of China's leading businesspeople, something it has done too many times in recent years. China still needs innovation and entrepreneurship from the 10 percent to drive job creation. They should not view the private sector as a necessary evil but as a key driver to improve the quality of life for the 90 percent through the creation of jobs.

China's tech crackdown must be viewed as a move by the government to create more competition and a fairer society and encourage entrepreneurship. As Deyu from the AI company we met in Chapter 2 said to me, "The tech crackdown is good for us. It means we do not have to take money from

Alibaba or Tencent and work within their ecosystems. The government is actively supporting us in AI. Instead of hurting us, the tech crackdown gives us more support and more opportunities to grow."

Deyu's sentiments were echoed by comments a billionaire private equity investor made to me over coffee in Shanghai: "The crackdown hurt a couple of players and will cause pain in the short term. But, in the long term, it will be good for other entrepreneurs, and it will increase their choice on whom they cooperate with. It will also force them to be more innovative and competitive. The government is really supporting these smaller internet players."

The sacrifice of a few for the benefit of the many is exactly what is happening with the tech crackdown. Ten percent of the overall population gets hurt while 90 percent of the population benefits. However, US media outlets like *The Wall Street Journal* and *Bloomberg* only interview members of the 10 percent, so their views are skewed and do not accurately reflect the sentiments of the population at large regarding the tech crackdown. Most of Chinese society, including tech entrepreneurs, support the tech crackdown. Most of Chinese society will benefit economically from the crackdown, unlocking their spending ability.

The crackdown not only creates more opportunities for the start-ups to become major players but also gives fatter margins to brands and restaurants and helps spur the growth of a larger middle class.

Poor communication

While there has largely been a misreading of the intentions behind the Chinese government's tech crackdown in the

Western investor community, there has been warranted criticism of how the government handled the crackdown in terms of speed and communication with the international investor community. Regulators should have better communicated the underlying reasons for the crackdown to the international (and even the domestic) investor community, including just how far and deep it would go. The lack of transparency has caused exaggerated fears that the government has become antibusiness, which has caused capital to flee the Chinese and Hong Kong equity markets.

Combined with a lack of communication to the international investor community, the crackdown was poorly implemented—the crackdown was too swift and cut too far to the bone. The crackdown scared entrepreneurs and innovators and destroyed animal spirits among the 10 percent. There was too much uncertainty over why the measures were taken, letting rumors abound that the goal of the crackdown was to clip the private sector and usher in an era akin to the Cultural Revolution when the government forged an antibusiness stand.

Private equity giant Warburg Pincus shut its TMT (technology, media, and telecom) and consumer teams for China. For years, Warburg had invested in some of the best technology companies in China, but for Warburg's heads in the US, the length and uncertainty of China's tech crackdown were too much to bear. Rumor also had it that LPs were shying away from Warburg's China-focused initiatives because of strong-arming by the US government not to back innovative Chinese tech companies.

As one private equity executive of a multibillion USD fund told me, "We are long-term bullish on the tech sector in China but we have not been able to find any good investments the last two years and do not expect to for several more—the cohort of tech companies just has not been good after the crackdown." Chinese entrepreneurs have delayed starting companies over fears of a fast changing policies. The government needs to return to the days when policymaking was stable and transparent in order to encourage the return of animal spirits

Profiting from the crackdown

Too often in recent years China's government has not clearly explained the underlying reasons for its crackdowns. The government needs to rebuild entrepreneur and investor confidence by being clear and transparent with their long-term goals and the underlying reasons for any investigations into companies or executives. Often, companies are placed under investigation, or executives are arrested or taken away to aid an investigation, without public announcements explaining why for months, sometimes years. In the meantime, investor confidence plummets and rumors send share prices plummeting.

While the days of the behemoth internet player, like Alibaba, controlling entire sectors and ecosystems are gone, the crackdown and resulting open competition will create more opportunities for little dragon start-ups in the tech space to become big dragons. The crackdown will also allow for better profit margins for companies like retailers and restaurants that use internet platforms to sell to consumers. SMEs profit from the crackdown and will be able to pay workers better, helping to create a vibrant middle class.

Joe, with whom we began this chapter, is wrong—China is still investable. Investors just need to understand what policy and regulatory changes mean for entire industries and specific sectors.

The days of monopolistic-like behavior by leading companies like Alibaba is over. Instead of a handful of behemoths, China will see the rise of many small dragons. Instead of being seen as a negative for businesspeople and investors, the tech crackdown should be viewed as a positive, and for two reasons. There is now a proliferation of new sales channels like Douyin, Red, and Pinduoduo for brands to sell their products and services on. Without the crackdown, these little dragons would not have been able to grow so quickly and take market share, as Alibaba dominated the entire ecommerce space. Brands also have more control over discounting and timing of discounts now that Alibaba no longer dominates and forces brands to discount. A more open playing field among sales channels will allow brands like Lululemon, Hoka, and On to earn fatter margins. Second, the end of Alibaba and Tencent's dominance has allowed start-ups to grow independently and be able to grab profits. Pinduoduo's market cap surpassed Alibaba's after the crackdown. Douyin has also emerged as a major platform for entertainment and ecommerce. The crackdown will allow new start-ups to become global players and give opportunities for investors to profit by backing new, innovative, and nimble companies.

Notes

1. Arjun Kharpal, "Ant Group to Raise $34.5 Billion, Valuing It at Over $313 Billion, in Biggest IPO of All Time," *CNBC*, October 26, 2020, https://www.cnbc.com/2020/10/26/ant-group-to-raise-tktk-billion-in-biggest-ipo-of-all-timehtml
2. https://mindmatters.ai/2021/01/chinese-entrepreneur-jack-ma-missing-after-criticizing-the-party/

3. Lulu Yilun Chen, "Fidelity, BlackRock Cut Fintech Giant Ant's Valuation Lower," *Bloomberg*, August 16, 2022, https://www.bloomberg.com/news/articles/2022-08-16/fidelity-blackrock-cut-fintech-giant-ant-s-valuation-further

4. Josh Dehaas, "China's Richest Man Jack Ma Says He Has 'Great Chemistry' with Trudeau," *CTV News*, September 25, 2027, https://www.ctvnews.ca/mobile/politics/china-s-richest-man-jack-ma-says-he-has-great-chemistry-with-trudeau-1.3605479?cache=yes%3FclipId%3D89925&referrer=https%3A%2F%2Fwww.google.com.hk%2F

5. Matt Levin, "Why Has China's Stock Market Been Struggling," *MarketPlace*, February 6, 2024, https://www.marketplace.org/2024/02/06/why-chinas-stock-market-struggling/

6. Julie Zhu and Kane Wu, "Canada's Largest Pension Fund Trims Staff as It Puts China Deals on Hold," *Reuters*, September 1, 2023, https://www.reuters.com/markets/canadas-largest-pension-fund-trims-staff-it-puts-china-deals-hold-sources-2023-09-01/

7. Song Jingli, "Meituan's Relationship with Dining Sector Sours as Covid-19 Tests Restaurants' Bottom Line," *KrASIA*, April 14, 2020, https://kr-asia.com/meituans-relationship-with-dining-sector-sours-as-Covid-19-tests-restaurants-bottom-line

CHAPTER 7

The Education and Training Crackdown

In one fell swoop as bloody as the Red Wedding in *Game of Thrones*, China's government decimated the for-profit education and training sector in the summer of 2021. Regulators moved to cap prices of tutoring sessions and limit what subjects could be taught in for-profit after-school programs. Subjects taught in the national education system became heavily regulated or outright banned in tutoring centers, from math to English to science. The government declared schools themselves should provide better training for students and that parents should not have to turn to expensive for-profit tutoring centers.

Wall Street shuddered at the new regulations. Stock prices of leading education companies like New Oriental plummeted by 70 percent overnight. Private equity investors saw multi-billion-dollar education investments evaporate. Executives in the sector I interviewed in the aftermath were close to tears—without any advance notice of the new regulations, all the work they had done over the years had disappeared in an instant. One teary-eyed entrepreneur, Pete, lamented, "I just can't believe it. I followed the law and look what happened: I am about to go out of business after spending seven years building my company."

Pete's training center offered classes in English starting at
250 USD per session, but he said the government told him
they would force him to cap classes at 30 USD per session.
"At these prices," he said, "I will be unable to make a profit."
He worried he would be forced to shut down and fire his
30 employees because he could not make payroll. "I'm planning on moving to Vietnam or another country more open
to the training sector and where policies do not change so
quickly," he cried. "China is just too risky with the changing
regulations."

I felt bad for Pete. He had done nothing wrong nor broken any laws. He had followed Chinese government regulations and catered to customer demands to teach English. In
dozens of interviews, I found parents and children reported
satisfaction with the quality of Pete's training One mother
told me she attributed her son's successful application to a
top American boarding school to Pete's training. Ultimately,
however, Pete's business model conflicted with Xi's Common
Prosperity drive—having classes that only the 10 percent
could afford is unfair in his Xi's China. Why should only the
rich be able to educate their children? As young married couples delayed or skipped having children, the government also
realized the high costs of educating children exacerbated the
low birth rate. To promote childbirths, the government has to
make raising a child more affordable for the 90 percent.

Pete planned to sell his stake in the business to someone
willing to operate with price caps. He was looking for buyers but found few serious takers as potential buyers remained
wary of the risks.

Despite parent and student satisfaction, Pete's business
model is no longer acceptable in Xi's China—services in sectors that the government deems a human right like education
cannot be allowed to create an uneven playing field for young

people. It is not fair that the 10 percent can equip their children with skills necessary for a better future while the 90 percent struggle to give their children educational opportunities.

The trend back toward socialism is clear. Businesses and investors cannot be blind to the shift and what that means for everything from pricing to the types of services offered—any businesses in sectors viewed as core to the needs of Chinese population like education must ensure their business models are not seen by the government as increasing economic inequality and preventing equal opportunities for social advancement. In those sectors, the political risk is high, as the government may well crack down without warning.

Getting ahead: anxiety and fear

The unheralded crackdown on the education sector understandably damages China's reputation among investors. Too many law-abiding companies like Pete's suddenly went bankrupt or faced hardship over sudden policy changes. A closer examination of the development of the training sector and an understanding of Xi's ideological underpinning shows why the sector was targeted.

Education and training companies like New Oriental and Xueda Education as well as smaller mom-and-pop chains made billions in profits off the backs of Chinese parents worried about their children's futures. Private equity firms like Sequoia Capital China, Warburg Pincus, and Hillhouse Capital invested billions backing start-ups in the training sector like Yunxuetang. Education and training was *the* sector to invest in, as the combination of anxious parents and a weak national education system meant big bucks for corporations that could help young Chinese get ahead of the competition.

As one wealthy Beijing mother lamented to me in 2014: "Competition for good jobs is so fierce, we have to spend a fortune on training for our 12-year-old daughter." The mother estimated she spent 60,000 USD a year on her daughter's math, English, painting, dance, ice-skating and horseback riding lessons. This was a price that few in China could afford. In 2014, the average per capita GDP in China was 7636 USD. In those go-go days, the government focused more on top-line economic growth than social equality, and so supported the proliferation of training companies targeting the wealthy.

In 2001, seeing the training sector as an opportunity, I too had founded an English training center in Tianjinin called the eponymous Little Mountain's English Training Center (my Chinese name means Little Mountain). The center taught English to five- to 14-year-olds whose parents wanted to equip them with English skills taught by native English speakers. In those days, a white face was all that was needed to teach English in many schools as parents were desperate for their children to learn from and interact with foreigners. Public schools even hired Russians with thick accents to teach English. My goal was to train children in proper spoken English. I even wrote a book, *Little Mountain's Guide on How to Get into Harvard*, to complement the training center, as I had dreams of turning the center into a training empire. Demand for "real" English training was so great we registered 137 students within our first hour of operation.

Ultimately, my business failed—the internet crawled in those days, so I was unable to scale my business. Rents were too high as developers controlled prime real estate, and I couldn't find foreign teachers willing to move to Tianjin. Despite my failure, there was clear market demand for learning English because parents worried so much about their children's futures.

Where I failed, however, savvier entrepreneurs figured out how to overcome the barriers. New Oriental offered large, lecture-style classroom settings where one teacher could teach hundreds of students at once, and later adopted e-learning as internet usage grew. Students and their parents who could afford their services were happy with the results because kids scored high on standardized tests and gained admission to international universities.

Private tutoring companies also sprouted up, offering a wide array of classes and extracurricular activities because parents considered the Chinese education system weak. Public schools often had 50 or more kids in a class. Textbooks and exams relied on rote memory and did not foster creativity.

As students rise through the Chinese system, their opportunity to get a liberal arts view of the world is also limited. When applying to domestic universities, applicants declare their majors during the application process. They have little flexibility in taking courses outside of their major. Finance majors essentially take four years of finance and nothing else. Biology majors spend four years taking biology classes. Too many of China's students are one-dimensional and do not have enough exposure to different disciplines or extracurricular studies.

The weak education system makes many parents willing to spend all their savings on extra training programs to help their children get into schools abroad. As one 50-something blue-collar worker from Qingdao told me, "I will borrow all the money I can if need be and use all my savings to send my daughter overseas to study if she can get in somewhere." He was skeptical of the Chinese education system so was willing to forfeit a secure retirement so his daughter could study abroad.

Over the past 40 years, millions of Chinese have left China to study in the US, UK, Australia, Canada, and Singapore, among other countries. In 2021 alone, despite Covid restrictions,

317,000 Chinese enrolled in American education institutions. Getting an overseas degree is viewed as a must-have ticket to career success and a good quality of life, especially as the sheer number of newly minted Chinese university graduates—over 10 million annually—entering employment every year means that there is fierce competition for the best, highest-paying, and most secure jobs. In the post-Covid era, youth unemployment in China rose to 21.8 percent for those between the ages of 18 and 24.

The Chinese government recognizes the weaknesses of the education system and has pushed for wider curricula and creativity in schools. They have adopted technology and engineering into their curricula. Xi has tried to turn China's leading universities such as Tsinghua and Peking into global leaders and recruited top Chinese academics to leave universities in America and Europe and return to China. Many of the reforms have worked, and several Chinese universities are ranked in the world's top 100 by the QS ranking system. Despite the reforms and improvements, for parents, there remains the fear that the reforms are too little and too late.

Studying abroad: the path to success

After China opened up in 1978, and until the early 2000s, the government supported Chinese students who chose to study abroad. The government wanted China's best and brightest to study overseas and bring back what they had learned to China to help reform the system, merging the best of the international system with Chinese culture and history in order to jumpstart the economy. Before my wife, Jessica, left for the US after graduating from the renowned international finance department at Renmin University in Beijing to pursue a Master's program in finance at Boston College, her grandmother, the famed actress Lili Li, told her to learn all she could so that she could return to China and help build and reform the finance system. Elite families wanted their children to learn from the American system's best practices not only so that they could get ahead in their own careers but also to bring back knowledge to China to help the country's wider reform efforts.

Many of China's top officials and businesspeople studied abroad and/or sent their own kids overseas. For example, party chairman Hu Yaobang's grandson attended Yale and Yale Law School; Vice Premier Liu He received a Master's degree at Harvard University; Baidu's founder, Robin Li, graduated from the University of Buffalo with a Master's after receiving his bachelor's from Peking University; Frank Wang, the founder of drone maker DJI, received his undergraduate degree from the Hong Kong University of Science & Technology (HKUST); and Colin Huang, the founder of ecommerce site Pinduoduo, graduated from the University of Wisconsin with a Master's degree after graduating from Zhejiang University with a bachelor's degree. Seeing the success so many of China's leading figures have had after graduating from overseas institutions, many Chinese parents want their kids to study abroad even if the costs are high. Getting a degree overseas also offers students the opportunity to work aboard, get global experience, and potentially even emigrate if the economic winds in China deteriorate.

Families in both the 10 percent and 90 percent continue to see a foreign education as the road to riches for their children, and this creates opportunities for foreign education institutions to attract Chinese students, education consulting firms that help students apply to schools abroad, and for foreign training companies that sell services online out of the reach of

Chinese regulatory crackdowns. An underground market of training services has opened throughout China with courses being taught one-to-one or in small groups in WeWork-like settings to get around rules banning physical training centers. The crackdown has actually caused prices to go even higher for the 10 percent.

Pressure from Party members

Pressure from within the Party itself to reduce education costs and create more opportunities for Party members and their families has also been an issue many analysts have omitted from their analysis of why the government has cracked down on education—the high costs of raising a child mean many top talents have decided to skip going into the Party to work in the government or in SOEs because they cannot afford to raise children if they do so. In other words, the high cost of education is hurting the Party's recruiting ability and causing anger within the ranks. Relatively low salaries combined with corruption crackdowns means that many Party members feel they can't take care of their families.

One 34-year-old Communist Party member, Anne, who works in an SOE in Beijing told me that the high cost of education was unfair. Her 39-year-old husband also works for the same SOE. Combined, they make about 5000 USD a month, which, while a relatively decent salary, still leaves her feeling worried about how she can afford to give her daughter the best opportunities.

She said, "I can't afford a good private school in Beijing for my six-year-old daughter which costs almost 50,000 USD a year, not including the cost of extra training sessions. It is so unfair." At the time, she sent her daughter to live with her husband's parents in his home province because tuition fees were so much cheaper there. Anne has thought about leaving her SOE job, a job she loves, to work in the private sector. Many of her colleagues, she told me, had already left to work in the private sector. Xi needs to focus not only on rejuvenating the Party to win the support of the masses but also on consolidating support from Party members like Anne. The education crackdown helps ensure Party members can afford to raise their children.

Lowering the overall costs of raising kids in order to encourage families to have more children has also become a priority as China faces an aging population. To alleviate its aging population, China's government abolished the one-child policy in late 2015, though since then only the rich have been able to take advantage of the policy change because the cost of raising a child is so high.

In 2021, China had a fertility rate (the average number of children born to a woman over her lifetime) of around 1.07,[1] and 10.62 million births, compared to 10.14 million deaths.[2] The situation is worse, even, than that in Japan where, in the same year, the fertility rate was 1.3, and there were 0.85 million births and 1.4 million deaths.[3] The fertility rates of both countries are at record lows. Most countries in the Western world have higher fertility rates: for example, in 2020 the US had a rate of 1.6 and in 2022 the UK's rate stood at 1.49.[4] In 2022, China's overall population dropped by 850,000 to 1.4118 billion, China's first decline in six decades. The overall national birth rate dropped to a record low of 6.77 births per 1000 people.

Couples are delaying marriage until their late twenties or early thirties, a trend most prominent in Tier 1 and Tier 2 cities, as salaries remain below expectations in the post-Covid era. This is very different from a generation ago when it was the norm for people to marry in their twenties. Many young people are also delaying getting married because they want a marriage of true love rather than one semi-formally arranged by their parents.

The lack of births and weddings poses a significant long-term threat to the labor and real estate markets. While automation or the potential import of workers from neighboring countries like Vietnam can help alleviate worker shortages, almost 90 million homes sit empty across the country. Without more babies, there won't be demand for these homes. Government caps on the price of training, as well as policies aimed at addressing health care access, are focused on eliminating two of the biggest barriers couples face in their decision about how many children to have.

Raising healthier and happier kids

The pressure on kids to succeed in school was enormous because families faced the high cost of paying for additional tutoring outside school. Parks were often devoid of children's laughter because kids were studying at home and in training centers until the wee hours. Kids had to study and succeed or else all the financial sacrifices their parents had made would be for naught.

One friend told me in 2018 that his 11-year-old daughter, Alice, studied until midnight every night. She had no time to play with friends and explore her creativity as she spent most of her time learning by rote memory. She was always indoors studying.

Until the crackdown on the education and training sectors, the quality of life for schoolchildren was poor and often impacted both their mental and physical health. The impact on health can be seen in the incidence of nearsightedness

among Chinese schoolchildren. In 2020, average nearsightedness rates in China for children below six years old was
around 14.3 percent, climbing to 35.6 percent of elementary-
school-aged children, before jumping to an astonishing 71.1 percent and 80.5 percent in middle-school and high school-aged
children.[5] For elementary-school children, their chances of
myopia increased 9.3 percentage points with every grade they
completed. Eyesight is such a problem in China that, when I
visited a classroom in Tibet, their teachers were leading eye
relaxation exercises to make sure students eyes were not too
tired.

China's crackdown on the training and education sector
sent shockwaves throughout the investment community, both
in China and the West, much as the tech crackdown did. Few
sectors have been left in such disarray or seen such a dramatic
evaporation of wealth in such a short period of time. At least
with the tech sector, companies like Alibaba and its subsidiary
Ant Financial were given the chance to reform and be regulated.
Although their profits have been clipped, these profit-making
machines have been allowed to remain in operation.

However, as with the tech sector, the reality on the ground
is that the government needed to crack down on the education
and training sector to benefit the 90 percent who had either been
unable to educate their children or had had to sacrifice their
retirement plans to do so. The government needed to ensure
that parents in the 90 percent group did not literally have to
mortgage their financial well-being just so their children could
be educated. Price caps on training classes or free ones offered
in schools after core hours will free up money for lower-income
Chinese to become middle class. They will begin to consume
more products and services and potentially have more babies.

The government also needed to ensure the quality of life
of Chinese youth so that they did not study too hard and

burn out. In fall 2022, I asked my neighbor's daughter, Alice, how school was. Her answered surprised me. Now, as a high-school student, I expected her to be studying and cramming to the wee hours so that she could get into a good university, but to my surprise my neighbor told me: "Great. Much less homework than before!" The government in 2023 even released a new regulation that schoolchildren should have at least two hours of outdoor exercise a day to reduce myopia and improve health and well-being.

While the crackdown on the education and training sector was poorly managed—it was too heavy-handed and cut too close to the bone—the majority of Chinese actually supported it. Lowering and capping training and education costs helps the 90 percent unlock their savings to spend on other categories (something I will explore later in the book). In other words, the crackdown will help grow the size of China's middle class and create more opportunities for foreign brands to sell into China.

For businesses, it is better to stay clear of investing in the education space in China. The risks of ongoing regulatory crackdowns are simply too high. Even providing education services via foreign-based websites is a risky business model as websites could be censored or blocked by China's Great Firewall. Businesspeople and investors can no longer focus only on market demands in China—they also have to ensure that their business models conform to the shift toward socialism that aims to reduce income inequality and benefit the 90 percent. For core sectors like education that the government views as a human right, fat margins are now a thing of the past.

Nonetheless, ongoing fears about China's weak education system despite the reforms, combined with unease among the 10 percent about the direction the country is taking, are creating opportunities for foreign businesses and international schools. Companies can benefit by selling SAT test prep to families who want to send their kids abroad to study, and foreign education institutions can attract more Chinese, especially among the 10 percent, who want their kids to seek better business opportunities abroad.

Notes

1. Kayleigh Bateman, "Birth Rates are Shrinking in Japan—and It's Part of a Worldwide Trend," *World Economic Forum*, January 31, 2022, https://www.weforum.org/agenda/2022/01/japan-global-birth-rate-decline/

2. Bill Conerly, "China's Birth Rate Not a Problem for Economy—Now," *Forbes*, January 22, 2022, https://www.forbes.com/sites/billconerly/2022/01/22/chinas-birth-rate-not-a-problem-for-economy-now/

3. Ryuichi Hisanaga, "Number of Births Plunging Faster Than Government Projections," *Asahi Shimbun*, June 3, 2022, https://www.asahi.com/ajw/articles/14636761

4. Heather Stewart, "Birthrate in UK Falls to Record Low as Campaigners Say 'Procreation a Luxury,'" *Guardian*, February 23, 2024, https://www.theguardian.com/uk-news/2024/feb/23/birth-rate-in-uk-falls-to-record-low-as-campaigners-say-procreation-is-a-luxury

5. Staff Writers, 2020 年我国儿童青少年总体近视率为52.7% 近视低龄化问题仍突出, *Xinhua News*, July 13, 2021, http://www.gov.cn/xinwen/2021-07/13/content_5624709.htm#:~:text=%E8%B0%83%E6%9F%A5%E7%BB%93%E6%9E%9C%E6%98%BE%E7%A4%BA%EF%BC%9A2020%E5%B9%B4,%E5%8F%91%E7%8E%B0%E8%B1%A1%E5%BE%97%E5%88%B0%E4%B8%80%E5%AE%9A%E7%BC%93%E8%A7%A3%E3%80%82

CHAPTER 8

Infrastructure

Planes, Trains, Subways, and Road Transportation

Riding his popularity as the supreme commander of the Allied Expeditionary Force during World War II, Dwight D. Eisenhower won the vote to become the 34th President of the United States in 1953. One of Eisenhower's first major acts—suggesting he was still thinking as a solider—was to push through the Federal-Aid Highway Act of 1956, also known as the National Interstate and Defense Highways Act. Originally intended to create a network of highways that could supply American troops in the event of a land war, the act had an alternative, longer-lasting effect—it fast-charged America's economic growth in post–World War II period by facilitating the shipping of goods nationwide and increasing connectivity between cities.

Small mom-and-pop businesses located in rural areas far from the commercial hubs of New York and Boston used the highway network to ship products from one end of the country to the other as well as to cater to new customers driving through. Small local businesses could grow into national conglomerates. Without Eisenhower's interstate highway system, Sam Walton never would have been able to build Walmart from a discount store in Rogers, Arkansas, a town with a population of only 5700 people, into a retailing goliath. Marriott International began its life in 1927 as a root beer stand in Washington, DC, but started along its path to becoming a global powerhouse in 1957 when it opened its first hotel, the Twin Bridges Motor Hotel, in Arlington, Virginia, exploiting its prominent site close to a highway to draw in vacationing families who needed a place to put their heads down for the night.

Eisenhower's highway system cut a cross-country trip from two months down to five days. Manufacturers could ship to retailers within days to locations that were convenient to American shoppers rather than them relying on the Sears catalog to buy something special. With the added transportation convenience, Americans started to move out of crowded inner cities to sprawling suburban compounds. The American dream of owning a house with a white picket fence and a car became accessible to millions of Americans for the first time because of Eisenhower's highway system.

During the 1980s, China's economic planners studied America and other countries like Germany, Japan, and South Korea to see what factors made their economies succeed. In those years of heady reforms, China focused on learning as much as it could from the West to jumpstart the economy. Ideas from any country and culture were acceptable as a discussion point. China simply wanted to learn best practices and then adapt them to suit China's history, culture, and geography.

China's economic planners wanted to know how countries, like Japan, South Korea, or Germany, rose from the ashes of all-out war to become economic juggernauts. Many commentators in America merely scratched the surface and attributed the growth to Confucian culture or a "Japanese way." China's economic planners dug deeper. They analyzed, for example, how Japan and South Korea had become manufacturing powerhouses and escaped the middle-income trap when average salaries hit 10,000 USD per capita. When countries hit that per capita GDP, economies often stall as comparative advantages and easy policy reforms are harder to find. China's planners knew China needed more than superficial cultural analysis and "fortune cookie" business advice to get its economy roaring again.

China's leaders realized that, for China to get out of poverty, it needed to initially follow two stages: first, to jumpstart economic growth by becoming the world's factory through export and, second, to grow through investment into infrastructure. Attracting investment from companies like Nike and Walmart would create factory jobs for millions of workers, lifting workers and their families out of the abject poverty of the 1970s.

Government officials realized that a low-cost labor pool was not enough incentive alone to attract money and to ensure manufacturing dominance in the long term. Nor was it enough to increase GDP over several decades—China needed to have an unparalleled infrastructure to ensure fast and stable shipment times as well as dole out tax breaks to attract foreign direct investment. After all, other countries like Vietnam, India, and Sri Lanka have even lower-cost labor pools than China but cannot grab major market share in manufacturing because they cannot compete with China's infrastructure.

China needed a combination of cheap labor and world-class infrastructure to attract manufacturing investment, especially as it moved past sanctions imposed on it after the Tiananmen Incident. The world had condemned China for the deaths of hundreds of students, so China needed to go above and beyond to reattract the world's capital by enabling foreign companies to cut down costs and become rich. China gave out preferential decade-long tax breaks to foreign companies while still forcing domestic Chinese companies to pay 25 percent profit taxes.

Leading infrastructure would allow manufacturers to ship products from factories to other countries by air, truck, and freight, and later within China once incomes rose. China embarked on a multi-decade initiative to upgrade not just ports, but also its train system, subways, and airports.

Starting its planning in the 1990s, China opened its high-speed rail network to increase the mobility of workforces and ensure shipping times. By 2022, China has invested an estimated 538 billion USD into its high-speed rail system that covers more than 37,900 km.[1] China's highspeed trains can travel up to 350 km/h.[2] To add some perspective, America's highest-speed train, the Amtrak Acela, has a maximum speed of 240 km/h but rarely touches such a high speed because the railroad tracks are winding, forcing locomotive drivers to go slowly.

In China, 9600 high-speed trains run every day compared to only 300 trains in the US (the countries are similar in size). China has over 5500 train stations that are often connected to its 235 airports and 4660 subway stations to enable seamless travel. China's high-speed train system is a technological marvel: fast, cheap, convenient, clean. The robustness of the high-speed train system has also allowed China not to be so beholden to Western aerospace companies Boeing and Airbus. While China has continued to buy jetliners from Airbus for political purposes, the high-speed trains have allowed China to become more independent of American and European technology in case of sanctions.

China's infrastructure spending on highways, ports, subways, and airports has proved a boon for job creation, interprovincial trade, and the construction of affordable housing—the necessary ecosystem required to maintain China's dominance in manufacturing as well as support its emerging services sector. China simply used Eisenhower's blueprint and improved upon it with the adoption and invention of new technologies such as elevated roads and high-speed trains.

No matter how much the US pressures corporate America to relocate its manufacturing and sourcing operations to other countries like Mexico, or even to re-shore back to America, China's infrastructure and tax breaks ensure that it will remain the factory of the world.

The nature of manufacturing and sourcing in China will change—it is no longer a cheap place to manufacture light industrial goods like apparel and footwear, so lower-end, more labor-intensive sectors will shift to Vietnam, Sri Lanka, Mexico, and other lower-cost production areas. China will remain dominant in high-precision and value-added manufacturing, continuing to take market share away from Germany where labor unions and high production costs are necessitating the relocation of manufacturing overseas. Even though Germany's chancellor Olaf Scholz is pushing German industry to de-risk from China, German CEOs, from Mercedes to Volkswagen, have ignored his pleas by investing billions into China in an effort to catch up to Chinese NEV makers. Volkswagen bought a 5 percent share in China NEV-maker Xpeng, and Mercedes CEO Ola Kallenius says cutting ties with China is "unthinkable."

Infrastructure spending not only facilitates business productivity but also enables workers to cut commute times to let them live in more affordable housing farther away from where they work. For example, when I studied at Nankai University in Tianjin in 1997, it was a three-hour train ride from Tianjin to Beijing. Now, it is only a 30-minute ride on a high-speed train between the two cities. It is common for people to live in Tianjin and work in Beijing; the train system allows the

Chinese people to realize the Chinese dream—owning nice homes in more affordable cities by commuting long distances to work in the same times frames at a low cost.

Roads at the top of the world

"Five years ago, it used to take 48 hours to drive from Lhasa to our small village," the slightly pudgy 42-year-old Tibetan man said as he showed me around the winding streets of his village. He was the village Communist Party secretary. He smiled. "Now it only takes 45 minutes." In the past five years, the government has built new roads and highways to connect the once-isolated village to the rest of Tibet to help villagers enter the modern economy.

The Party Secretary motioned me to enter the courtyard of one of the villager's homes—a towering two-story villa with an outdoor courtyard to welcome guests. This type of home would easily cost 5–10 million USD in Shanghai but looked to be a common house design in the village; I could see similarly sized villas with courtyards lining the entire main street.

I could not believe the speed of change that had turned this previously out-of-the-way village into a tourist destination. I had just driven from Lhasa to the village, a smooth 45-minute ride on a modern highway system as good as, if not better than, any I had encountered in America. The changes that infrastructure spending had brought to this Tibetan village — once one of the poorest in Tibet, an official told me—were mind-boggling.

From two days to 45 minutes, and in just five years! I could not help but compare this to Boston's Big Dig construction project that had stretched over decades from when I was a little kid until I became an adult—and with massive cost overruns.

"The roads and short commute time have opened up a whole world of business opportunities for the people of my village," the Party secretary beamed. "We were so poor here until the government built the highway from Lhasa to our village."

The Party secretary described the economic benefits the roads had brought to the village. Using the roads for transportation, villagers grew more crops like peaches that they sold before they spoiled. Cold chain delivery was becoming a reality in Tibet, allowing produce to be shipped all over the country in refrigerated trucks rather than in the back of open-aired trucks that limited shipping distances.

Some Tibetan peasants use live streaming on Taobao and Douyin to sell products like walnuts and incense to other provinces in China, my guide told me. A whole cottage industry had emerged with peasants and factories owners making vignettes to upload onto video sites to sell products or to earn tips from viewers of live-streaming shows.

The new highway system had also allowed the village to open up a hot springs hotel to attract the booming domestic Chinese tourism that viewed Tibet as a spiritual or relaxing destination. As I toured the hot spring hotel, I saw droves of Han Chinese frolicking in the water, taking videos amid Tibet's stunning mountain landscape.

Tibet's newly built highway system has revolutionized Tibet's economy—when I first visited Tibet in 2001, life looked as though it had not changed for centuries. The vice general manager of an incense factory in another village told me, "Five years ago, the majority of our incense was shipped a few kilometers from our factory. Now over 70 percent is shipped out of Tibet to other parts of China because of the road systems." He proudly picked up one of his packages printed with multiple languages and said that he had even started shipping to Europe. He uses Alibaba's Taobao and other ecommerce platforms to sell his wares.

"Perhaps even more importantly than attracting new tourist dollars," the village Party secretary said, "the government has also paved the streets of our village. It used to take my children three hours every day to walk to elementary school on dirt paths. But because of the paved roads, it's now a seven-minute school bus trip. Thanks to government infrastructure spending, my kids can now go to school easily."

After visiting the peasant's home, the Party secretary took me to a peach orchard where you could pick your own fruit. There were dozens of tourists from all over China visiting, including a group of young adults from Gansu Province. They were taking selfies to share on social media.

After my time picking peaches, I interviewed a 25-year-old college graduate born in the village who now worked at the hot spring hotel. He had studied in Jiangsu Province in China's eastern coastal region and worked there for one year. He told me that he came back to the village because the salaries working at the hot spring hotel were almost the same as those for jobs working in the big coastal cities of China. Back home, his housing costs were around 5 percent of the cost he faced in big cities. He also no longer felt as though he needed to be in a big city to get access to decent health care. He was happy, too, because he could be with his family now on a daily basis rather than see them only once a year during the Chinese New Year Spring Festival holiday. For him, the combination of decent salary, low-cost housing, accessible health care, and having his family close by meant it was a no-brainer to return to his native region.

This trend of workers returning to their home provinces because of the opportunities afforded by infrastructure spending is increasing: the costs of living in Tier 1 cities are too high. Moreover, the quality of life in lower-tier cities is similar to that of Tier 1 cities now as more chain restaurants and stores open up and as the ecommerce system now brings the same products to the countryside. This reverse migration to hometowns in the countryside due to the better job opportunities now on offer there, combined with unhappiness over Covid restrictions, helps explain why the population of Guangdong—a coastal province—dropped by 272,000 to 126.57 million in 2022.[3]

Over the next several decades, more companies in search of lower costs will relocate their operations to China's poorer regions such as Inner Mongolia, Henan, and Tibet as they improve their infrastructure capability. China has also eased the household registration system known as *hukou* in all but the largest cities in the country. This will allow Chinese to buy homes in these cities and send their kids to school there. The infrastructure rollout has allowed large companies to relocate their manufacturing from Guangdong Province to areas closer to where their workers are originally from—this has already happened with Foxconn and Intel. Foxconn relocated 300,000 workers from Shenzhen (China's third most populous city) to Henan Province where it now makes most of the world's iPhones. Intel has built huge manufacturing facilities in Chengdu in the western province of Sichuan. Honeywell has opened a major research and design center in Wuhan, Hubei Province. Airbus located a major manufacturing plant in Tianjin that might be its most advanced globally.

Through lower costs and tax breaks, China's government entices privately funded company operations and forces state-owned enterprises (SOEs) to help build up lower-tier cities and create a reverse migration from top-tier cities back to these poorer regions. China's infrastructure spending allows for the migration to happen while keeping economic competitiveness.

China's infrastructure spending means employees will be able to find better accommodation farther from offices but have the same commute times and live closer to their hometowns. The buildup of new cities and districts creates opportunities for brick-and-mortar businesses like KFC to continue opening new locations where new neighborhoods spring up.

The quality of life in these once-poor regions is getting better, causing Chinese workers to return home to find work. They no longer want to live hundreds of miles away from their families, seeing them only once or twice a year. The apprentice to my son's orthodontist in Shanghai actually left and moved back to Wulumuqi, Xinjiang, to seek his fortune there, because living costs were so much cheaper. He regularly posts pictures of his travels around Xinjiang on WeChat Moments, with comments on how cheap everything is.

China's coastal Tier 1 cities will remain vibrant economically, but the big growth opportunities are no longer in these cities. The real growth moving forward is in lower-tier cities that are growing because infrastructure spending allows for new development. The lower rents will attract more businesses looking to invest.

By investing in infrastructure, education and health care, lower-tier cities offer a greater quality of life at a fraction of the cost. Over the next ten years, reverse migration back to cities like Baotou, Inner Mongolia, will occur, as we have already seen in neighboring Ordos. It is in this context that China's public infrastructure spending should be viewed as a public good, rather than purely as a money-making enterprise. Indeed, many of China's subway and high-speed train networks lose money and need to be subsidized by local governments—to the tune of over a billion USD a year in some cities like Beijing. But the benefits they bring to the overall economy cannot be underestimated.

With lower costs and ease of transportation, companies can rethink the locations of their headquarters. They no longer need to be located in the downtown or even the main Central Business District (CBD) of Tier 1 cities. New CBDs are being built in cities across China and are being connected by sprawling metro systems enabling employees to commute. Companies can save on rent by moving to cheaper locations within a city, or even to neighboring cities that are being connected by highways, metros, and high-speed rail.

Workers in lower-tier cities are the most optimistic in the country today as they are able to buy affordable housing yet still get paid good wages. The result is that growth in consumer spending will come from Tier 3–Tier 5 cities rather than from Tier 1 cities like Shanghai and Beijing. Companies selling into China need to take advantage of the urbanization into these new areas by opening up points of sale and utilizing ecommerce delivery networks to target the newly emerging Chinese consumer class.

China's infrastructure spending will enable it to maintain its dominance in manufacturing and increasingly allow it to grab a share in global services. The combination of low-cost living and ease of transportation will allow Chinese service firms to become more profitable. This is why China is giving rise to large companies that got their start in Tier 3–Tier 5 cities—they are becoming like the new Marriotts and Walmarts of the 21st century that benefit from infrastructure spend.

Notes

1. Staff Writers, 年年亏钱年年建，高铁的意义何在"酷玩实验室, February 7, 2021, https://www.163.com/dy/article/G282G6140 511BCOA.html

2. Ben Jones, "Past, Present and Future: The Evolution of China's Incredible High-Speed Rail Network," *CNN*, February 9, 2022, https://www.cnn.com/travel/article/china-high-speed-rail-cmd/index.html

3. Staff Writers, "Guangdong Sees First Population Decline in Over Years," *Macau News Agency*, April 23, 2023, https://www.macaubusiness.com/guangdong-sees-first-population-decline-in-over-40-years/

CHAPTER 9

Supply Chains

Looking beyond China to India, Vietnam, and Mexico

One sweltering day in 2003, I sat down in a five-star hotel overlooking Hong Kong's gleaming harbor to meet with Rick, the chief executive officer of Acme Corporation. Established in the US Deep South near cotton plantations, Acme was a company with a 200-year history that was looking to enrich its shareholders. Every discussion we had focused on how to relocate manufacturing operations to China to generate profits for shareholders—in the self-interested, Ayn Rand way that pushed American business at the turn of the millennium. He salivated at how monthly salaries in China were only 100–200 USD a month, a fraction of salaries in the US.

A few months earlier, I had joined a venture capital (VC) firm to look after technology and education investments and oversee due diligence for potential investments. At that time, many American companies were looking to take advantage of China's entry into the World Trade Organization (WTO) in 2001 to relocate manufacturing from America to China to save costs, and this in turn created opportunities for those advising American firms on what to do.

One of my bosses in the VC firm, Jumbo, decided to open a subsidiary consulting firm that helped American companies shift their sourcing operations to China. Because of my research skills, he seconded me to the consulting firm. Jumbo hated communists so much he might have popped out of a McCarthy-era cartoon. He thought communism was evil by definition. But now he was willing to do business in "red China" and with "commies" just to make money.

Despite having lived in Asia for 30 years, Jumbo knew very little about China, so turned to junior people like me to do the work. That is how I ended up sitting with the global CEO of Acme, helping him salvage his company, even though I knew nothing about metal fasteners or manufacturing.

"Shaun," Rick said, "Our business is in trouble. We've been selling products since the Civil War to denim companies like Levi's. But because of China's entry into the WTO, the entire manufacturing sector has left the US and moved to China."

Rick then told me how entire industries and entire economic ecosystems had shifted from the US and Europe to China. Once a halo company like Levi's had relocated to China, everyone else in the supply chain had to join them or else they would get replaced by the competition. Zipper companies like Japan's YKK, the label companies ... companies all along the value chain like Rick's had to move to China and follow Levi's or risk irrelevance or bankruptcy at home.

Acme Corporation faced bankruptcy as they were already two years behind their competitors in relocating to China. Because of the delay, Acme was being outcompeted by companies from Taiwan, Hong Kong, Japan, and, increasingly, mainland China. Acme's sales sputtered, and its valuation had plummeted so much they had been acquired by a New York-based private equity firm that focused on buying and turning around distressed assets.

Acme's private equity owners pressured Rick to move manufacturing to China because of its cheap labor to salvage the business. Rick had engaged us to help the company build a factory and develop new sales channels.

"The reality," Rick said, "was that many manufacturing companies in America were already on the verge of bankruptcy, even before the shift of manufacturing to China." He told me, because of high labor costs, the difficulty of finding workers willing to slave and toil at hard factory work, and a lack of incentives, the American manufacturing industry was in peril. American firms like Acme had to relocate to China or else they would go bankrupt.

Trying to avert bankruptcy at the turn of the millennium triggered a rush to search for cheap labor in China. Outsourcing there created short-term dislocation in the labor markets in American and Europe. From 1965 and 2000, the average number of manufacturing jobs in the US held firm at 17 million according to the OECD, but between 2000 and 2010, America lost 5.8 millions of those jobs.[1]

"For Acme, Shaun, it's do or die. We must move to China or else we will go out of business for good," Rick told me.

Helping Acme avert bankruptcy is how I found myself with Jack and his underlings planning a new manufacturing facility in Guangdong Province. Over the next year, we found the land for the new factory, oversaw construction, and hired staff. Ultimately, Acme's shift to China worked well.

Acme's private equity owners made millions, and Jumbo got his big fat consulting fees despite having to deal with hated communists. Chinese got jobs that could help feed their families, even if the salaries were low. Acme's American workers in their factories back in Georgia did lose jobs but they benefited from cheaper, made-in-China products and eventually found work elsewhere.

Acme's successful restructuring led its private equity firm owners to buy more faltering American brands and relocate them to China, earning huge profits for them and their American investors.

Acme's success is representative of the symbiotic trade relationship between China and the US in the early years after China entered the WTO. The prevailing wisdom of policymakers like President Bill Clinton was that China's economic rise brought profits to American industry. They supported outsourcing to make money for American shareholders and to push for China to become a liberal democracy. Aside from the American factory worker in the short term, everyone benefited from the trade relationship—American investors and brands made billions of profits, and Chinese workers got much needed jobs.

As you can see from Acme's case, the reality is China did not steal or cheat when it captured manufacturing market share, as it is popular for Trump and other American politicians scavenging for votes like to say. In truth, China outcompeted the US and Europe by offering the mix of low-cost labor and some of the best infrastructure in the world. American firms and their investors decided to take advantage of these low costs to relocate supply chains to China in the search for profits.

And profit they did. Profiting from manufacturing in China is why trade associations like the American Apparel & Footwear Association (AAFA) and the American Chamber of Commerce in Shanghai criticized Trump's and Biden's trade war and their 300 billion USD worth of tariffs on Chinese goods. AAFA president Rick Helfenbein wrote a letter to President Trump saying that "[Tariffs have] caused severe damage to US companies, the millions of US workers they employ and the hundreds of millions of US consumers they service."[2] Relocating manufacturing to China also helped the American consumer increase their savings and spending power. Since China entered the WTO, the average US household has more money to spend on products from places like Amazon or Walmart because of the low cost of the "Made in China" label.[3] Without China's low-cost manufacturing, Americans would not have been able to afford the iPhones and Nike shoes they buy today.

The trade relationship was not unbalanced. China also benefited from the trade. China was desperate for job creation even if it caused pollution, as we saw in the chapter on rare earths. Even if manufacturing shoes, toys, and shirts caused pollution, it was worth it just to create jobs and put food on the tables of the Chinese people.

China soon dominated global manufacturing, becoming known as the "world's factory," and thereby gained leverage over other nations. By 2021, 30 percent of all manufacturing output came from China.[4] War hawks in the Trump regime like Peter Navarro, director of the White House National Trade Council, and Robert Lighthizer, US Trade Representative, did not like having so much of America's industry outsourced to a nation they viewed as threatening American interests. They executed Trump's trade war to reduce America's reliance on China for manufacturing.

Controlling the manufacturing of antibiotics, toys, and auto parts meant China could not easily be pressured in geopolitical affairs. China's control of key supply chains gave it leverage over the US, in much the same way Putin's control of LNG had given Russia leverage over Europe. Its drive to control the global supply chain to maintain leverage is why China will continue to offer incentives and keep building infrastructure in order to bolster its manufacturing dominance—not only does manufacturing dominance create jobs and profits for China, but it also serves as leverage over the US. This was leverage that Japan had until it agreed to the Plaza Accord and thus lost much of its independence from American foreign policymaking.

China's manufacturing dominance is an area that Trump and Biden wanted to challenge with their trade wars, but not because of an unfair balance of trade, IP protection issues, or any other of the red herrings American officials pointed to—simply, America did not want to continue to enrich a rival economy that could soon eclipse America in power and which it no longer had much leverage over. As long as most of the key products Americans love and need are made in China, the Chinese can withstand pressure from America to conform to its political wants.

As the early 2010s dawned, China became less welcoming toward the low-end, high-polluting manufacturing that had dominated the first wave of American offshoring of labor to China. This now typically moved on to Vietnam, Sri Lanka, and other, even lower-cost manufacturing areas. Chinese workers were no longer as desperate for jobs and demanded higher salaries. China's newly minted middle class, as we will see in the next chapter, started to get angry at the pollution enveloping the country from light industry. Xi had just become president, and he no longer wanted the type of manufacturing and unintended consequences like pollution that Acme brought to China. The work was too unskilled, the pollution too high, and the salaries too low.

Instead, Xi wanted to bring high-end manufacturing to China like auto, medical equipment, and aerospace. One of the sectors most welcomed in China to help rework its growth playbook is now advanced, high-precision manufacturing such as robotics and companies in the NEV supply chain that pay high salaries and emit low pollution while still enabling China to maintain enough dominance in manufacturing to have leverage over the US. Unless banned by

America, companies that manufacture in advanced, highly technical and value-added sectors should continue operations in China because they receive tax benefits and subsidies and get to use China's best-in-class manufacturing ecosystem. No other country can provide the ecosystem necessary for such value-added manufacturing at such cheap prices. However, because of the threats of more American tariffs and other protectionist policies, these companies should not expand operations in China but expand to other countries like Mexico and Vietnam that are favored by American politicians. This is the so-called "China Plus One" strategy.

The "Made in China" risk

Educated at a US university, Bob is a Taiwanese American entrepreneur who lived in Shanghai for 15 years. While in China, he started a successful company selling consumer electronics into the country and became a member of the Young Presidents' Organization (YPO). Seeing the rising trend toward health and wellness globally after Covid hit the world, Bob started a medical device company to cater to the desire of consumers to live healthier lifestyles. But as he built up his company—he told me over coffee one day—he started to worry about manufacturing in China if he wanted to sell into the American and European markets. China's zero-Covid policies made shipping times to international markets slow, costly, and unstable if any factories got locked down. He needed a backup plan.

Bob decided to uproot his family and move to Taipei. He wanted to base his entire operations and supply chain in Taiwan, from headquarters to manufacturing, because of political calculations and rising political risk from America for any China-made products

After all, Bob believed the US would be his biggest market, and he was scared that, if he had the "Made in China" label on his products, or if his headquarters were located in mainland China, American companies would not buy from him or that tariffs would be slapped on his goods. He also thought that saying to potential clients that his entire product range was produced in Taiwan, a Western-style liberal democracy, would be a good selling point to American companies that bought along ideological lines.

Bob also knew mainland customers buy products with the "Made in Taiwan" label out of patriotism since they consider Taiwan part of China. The Chinese government, too, supports increased economic integration between the mainland and Taiwan to help make reunification more palatable and inevitable. China has always opened the red carpet to Taiwanese to invest on the mainland, especially in Fujian Province, which lies across the Taiwan Strait. SOEs and private Chinese companies would therefore buy products made in Taiwan. Bob told me, "I am worried we will get hit with high tariffs in the US or be banned outright if we source from the mainland, so I moved my entire operations to Taiwan."

Determining where to expand supply chains because of political risk—from the American, not the Chinese, side—is a problem faced by company after company because of tariffs and geopolitical uncertainty. American politicians are becoming protectionist and willing to slap tariffs on "Made in China" high-tech products, a sector the country is beginning to dominate, from NEVs to telecom equipment. As a result, any cost savings by manufacturing in China might disappear if tariffs are levied.

Ultimately, Bob told me, he was right to be concerned. One of his US distributors sold to military-run hospitals in the US and wanted nothing to do with China. They required country of origin labeling for every single part of the product and anything with the "Made in China" label got looked upon with disfavor by procurement officials. They wanted products made in the US or in democracies with good ties with the US like Taiwan. In an age of de-risking, the "Made in China" label has become a liability when selling to many American B2B companies that want to cut anything made in China out of the supply chain.

Despite pressure from America to contain China's manufacturing dominance, however, China won't lose its control anytime soon. This is not only because of the country's superlative infrastructure and tax breaks, but because the China market itself it too big and alluring—Bob told me he had decided to start manufacturing on mainland China in addition to Taiwan. As Chinese began spending more money on health and wellness after the Covid era, Bob realized the mainland market for his medical devices was massive. To get products to Chinese quickly and at affordable rates, Bob realized he also needed to set up a supply chain specifically for the mainland market. He did this not because mainland customers would spurn the "Made in Taiwan" label but because of the ease and speed of shipping from Guangdong to all over China.

Bob decided to create two supply chains:

1. one in Taiwan to sell to his American client base

2. another in mainland China to sell to the Chinese market.

Bob's experiences show companies must source and manufacture close to the end consumer—the speed of companies like Shein and Temu that can bring a product from factory to the homes of customers within days means that companies can no longer rely on long delivery times of months or even weeks.

Companies should build new sourcing supply chains outside of China in case political tensions rise, but they can't abandon manufacturing in China outright because no other country can replace China as the world's factory. They also need to manufacture in China to sell into China. If foreign companies do not have some China-based manufacturing for China at a minimum, they will cede market share to fast-moving Chinese brands that only manufacture in China and sell into China.

The future of manufacturing in China

Despite China rolling out the red carpet for high-end manufacturing companies like Bob's, companies face political risk from the US if they manufacture in China. Biden has tried to convince American companies not to invest in China through a mix of carrots and sticks and is strong-arming American companies not to keep investing in China in higher-value-added sectors like semiconductors (as we saw in Chapter 4) by banning them from selling products and services to Chinese firms.

The US–China trade war has made companies rethink whether it is still viable to manufacture in China or whether they should relocate to lower-cost options like Vietnam, Mexico, or India that are supported by the US government. What is clear is that companies need to factor in political risk from both China and the US when planning enlargement of their sourcing operations, which will also all be done for most sectors and most products outside of the US. Looking for an excuse for their criticisms of China to sell to the American public, Trump and Biden complained about the trade balance deficit and that China was taking unfair advantage of the US, so they slapped tariffs against China. Biden and Trump both encouraged sourcing from other nations like Vietnam, India, and Mexico where they were looking to gain more influence and offset rising Chinese power. In 2023, Mexico replaced China as America's largest trade partner. Despite the new supply chain patterns, my firm, CMR, estimates the overall trade deficit with China has not dropped since Trump started the trade war. The overall trade deficit was clearly not the problem causing America to employ economic coercion and sanctions on China—the problem was that China had gotten too strong and started to sap power away from America. For the national security crowd and war hawks like Navarro, a strong China by definition is a security threat.

Reshoring back to the US or to Germany is not really an option for most companies because it is too expensive to produce in America, with its high labor costs and taxes and tight environmental regulations. Only the most powerful and strategically necessary companies, like Taiwan's semiconductor giant TSMC, which announced a 50 billion USD investment program at a signing ceremony between Biden and TSMC founder Morris Chang in Arizona, will get the red-carpet treatment necessary to make manufacturing in the US plausible.[5] Even with Biden's support, TSMC saw labor unrest with workers saying there is too much pressure and not enough pay. As a result, TSMC has tried to send workers from Taiwan over to its US plants, increasing the tension between line workers and corporate officers.

Companies do need to diversify their supply chains to lessen the risk of black swan disruptions like Covid in addition to the rising political risk. I usually recommend, as a minimum, having two supply chains set up near end customers, just as Bob did with his medical device company. Companies could set up a supply chain in China to sell into China, a supply chain to sell into the US, and potentially a third one that can supply both regions as a backup. The cost of running multiple supply chains is high, but is worth it because of the very real risk of having your entire supply chain in one country, where it is vulnerable to war, another pandemic like Covid, or a round of sanctions.

If companies do not have backup supply chains, they could miss earnings targets if they get hit by supply chain disruptions. Apple, for instance, put too much of its production in Zhengzhou, Henan, at the Foxconn factory. Apple's iPhone 14 Pro supply dropped by 6 million units in the fourth quarter of 2022 because of Foxconn's factory closures in October and November owing to Covid containment policies. Apple should have had backup plans in place where it could shift production to other countries. Apple is now diversifying its manufacturing facilities to India and Vietnam to prevent another total breakdown of its supply chain.

Today, the world is splitting—in response to pushback against globalization and as America seeks to neutralize threats to an American-led world order. In the short term, The Split will be costly for both America and China as companies have to waste money setting up multiple supply chains, thereby hitting their profits. However, in this highly charged geopolitical environment, companies must adjust to political realities and diversify their supply chain risk. Companies need to create manufacturing hubs near where the end customer is.

Notes

1. William B. Bonvillian, "US Manufacturing Decline and the Rise of New Production Innovation Paradigms," *OECD*, 2017, https://www.oecd.org/unitedstates/us-manufacturing-decline-and-the-rise-of-new-production-innovation-paradigms.htm

2. Huileng Tan, "US Industry Leader on Tariffs: 'Prices Will Go Up, Sales will Go Down, Jobs Will Be Lost,'" *CNBC*, August 24, 2018, https://www.cnbc.com/2018/08/24/trade-war-tariffs-may-mean-prices-go-up-sales-go-down-jobs-are-lost.html

3. Staff Writers, "China Accounts for 30 percent of Global Manufacturing Output in 2021," *The State Council Information Office, The People's Republic of China*, June 15, 2022, http://english.scio.gov.cn/m/pressroom/2022-06/15/content_78271432.htm

4. Ana Swanson, "Biden Administration Releases Plan for $50 Billion Investment in Chips," *New York Times*, September 6, 2022, https://www.nytimes.com/2022/09/06/business/economy/biden-tech-chips.html

5. Tristan Bove, "How Many iPhones Will Apple Lose from a Covid Lockdown at the Biggest Factory in the World? How About 6 Million, Bank of America Says," *Fortune*, November 8, 2022, https://finance.yahoo.com/news/many-iphones-apple-lose-covid-213031642.html?guccounter=1&guce_referrer=aHR0cHM6Ly93d3cuZ29vZ2xlLmNvbS8&guce_referrer_sig=AQAAADzlUO9w-J2QqTEP6xR92ySKfub2gAqrn1m-WAGgz862JGRZKV-ll2CvVIhRHCUJt2sV9eUnBFrMMuKAPKN1xTgdJ3lDAagwl1F-DGCh7y_3TrlhbHV3sWOluZtOsKIiDZhY4WcI20XbG96ag-qtuDyvo7ZxFsWILDInCmBBFttWfOX

CHAPTER 10

Reducing China's Carbon Footprint and Pollution

By the early 2010s, corruption and pollution posed the greatest threats to the legitimacy of the Communist Party of China (CPC). Citizens dealt with corruption on a daily basis, creating much frustration in society—it might be a bribe given to a policeman to get out of a speeding violation, an ATM card with a very healthy account handed to a procurement official to seal the deal, or a wad of cash given to a doctor to secure an appointment or ensure incisions are made with care.

Endemic corruption made the Chinese angry as it favored the 10 percent, an anger that made the CPC lose popular support among the 90 percent. Without a vote to gain legitimacy, the Party has to rely on being seen as doing good for the country to maintain support of the 90 percent. Government corruption ate away at support and made the Chinese joke cynically that many officials went into the Party to enrich themselves rather than to help the country.

Buildings were often so poorly built that former prime minister Zhu Rongji compared them to tofu. Tragically, 5335 schoolchildren perished during the 2008 Sichuan Earthquake in large part because of shoddy school construction that passed safety inspections by corrupt officials.[1] Patients died or became ill when medical officials green-lighted medicines of dubious qualities because they were bribed.

Wide-ranging and regular anticorruption campaigns were used to ensnare senior officials and thereby regain public support for the Party. Despite the corruption crackdowns, to everyday Chinese, it seemed as though nearly every province and every city had at least one senior leader complicit in corruption. Were the ones arrested only those unlucky enough to be caught? the 90 percent thought. Were the ones arrested just part of the wrong faction, detained not because they were corrupt but because they were on the losing side of a power struggle?

Deep as the public's frustration with such endemic corruption was, China's pollution problems caused even more widespread anger starting in the early 2010s. The Chinese were no longer desperate just to put food on the table but also started to focus on health and wellness. While anyone with enough money could get ahead if they bribed their way to lucrative deals, pollution impacted every Chinese person, no matter how rich or well connected. Pollution soiled every inch of land, blackened the lungs of every child and elderly person. There was no way to hide from the noxious dark clouds that hung in the skies, not just in cities but in the countryside. Everyone from the peasantry to the elite suffered from airborne particulates, toxic water runoff from factories, or from food raised in contaminated soils. Asthma, bronchitis, and other respiratory ailments burdened the health care system. Parents worried for the health and futures of their children.

To minimize the ill effects of pollution, Chinese bought air purifiers for their homes and started wearing masks on a daily basis. Few ventured outside for sports like running and soccer. The popularity of indoor sports like basketball soared as people gasped for air when exerting themselves outside. Street food and market vendors suffered as consumers flocked to giant malls where they could spend the whole day indoors shopping, eating, and watching movies without exposing themselves directly to the outdoor air. Rather than visit domestic beauty spots where the skies were grey, tourists ventured to blue-air destinations like Thailand and Bali to escape China's black skies

Jon Stewart of *The Daily Show* joked one could chew Beijing's air. For a global superpower on the rise, China's pollution problems became a national embarrassment for the government.

Tackling pollution

As soon as he took the leadership helm from Hu Jintao, Chairman Xi tackled the two main issues hurting CPC legitimacy with a force few expected. Under Xi, the CPC launched a relentless, decade-long crackdown on corruption that went to the very top. In 2014, the Party arrested China's security chief and member of the standing committee of the Politburo, Zhou Yongkang.[2] He was later jailed for life, found guilty of taking over 20 million USD in bribes, although rumors abounded that his wealth had in fact reached into the billions.

With equal ferocity Xi also pushed to reduce China's carbon footprint, improve the environment, and focus on renewable energy as a new growth driver for the economy. Xi implemented higher standards of gasoline for vehicles despite pushback from the state-owned oil industry and pushed the adoption of NEVs through tax breaks and other subsidies. China overtook Japan to become the largest exporter of automobiles, many of them NEVs. By pushing for the adoption of NEVs, China not only reduced pollution but also began to control a new technology supply chain, encompassing not only automotive companies like BYD, Li Xiang, and NIO but innovatory battery companies like CATL. These new growth drivers reduce pollution and spur sustainable economic growth.

The government also shut pollution-belching factories and forced companies to adopt the highest environmental standards. The government announced its aim to reach net-zero emissions by 2060 and supported renewable energy sources like wind and solar, as well as nuclear power. Stringent pollution controls forced factories to shut or relocate to Vietnam, Ethiopia, and other markets with lower environmental standards.

By combatting pollution and corruption, Xi created a groundswell of support for the CPC and himself among the 90 percent, thereby rejuvenating the Party. The 90 percent felt they could trust the CPC with Xi at the helm to do the right thing for them and for the Motherland. Xi has made their children healthier and the economy run more smoothly and without the day-in, day-out corruption. Xi's leadership restored trust in the CPC that had been dwindling because of the growing social discontent and income inequality that had marred the previous decade.

Gaining popular support remained critical for Xi as he realized he needed to shore up patriotism at home in order to combat the growing tension with America—without that popular support, Xi and the Party would not be able to withstand a slowing economy under threat from a broken growth model and from American economic sanctions.

Shutting high-polluting factories

Over a dinner of barbequed Korean beef, I spoke to Mr. Lee, the CEO of a large South Korean manufacturing company that makes thread for the apparel sector. He complained to me about being forced to relocate his factories out of China to Vietnam. He was not happy about the forced move because of the costs and lost manufacturing time incurred.

The local government in Jiangsu Province had given him a stark choice—spend millions of dollars in pollution reduction or shut his factory completely and leave China. Before then, Mr. Lee had not given a moment's thought to pollution runoff from his factories—his focus was entirely on manufacturing his thread at as low a cost as possible. Besides, he did not even live in China so did not really care about the pollution spewing from his factories. Many of the worst polluters were factories owned not by mainland businesspeople but ones from Taiwan, Hong Kong, South Korea, and Japan. They did not live in China itself so they spent as little as possible on environmental protection.

Mr. Lee decided to relocate his operations to Vietnam, where environmental standards were laxer. The cost would be too high to upgrade his factories on the mainland. It was cheaper just to build new ones in Vietnam.

Mr. Lee's experience is not uncommon in the manufacturing sector. By the early years of Xi's administration, local officials gave companies the choice either to upgrade their factories with antipollution equipment and measures or be forced to shut and relocate. The government shifted away from a policy of job creation and investment at all costs to sustainable economic growth. No longer were high-polluting factories in Tier 1 cities like Beijing and Shanghai simply moved to poorer regions of China as they were in the 1990s. Relocating factories to poorer regions was obviously not a sustainable strategy, as it simply moved the problem to another part of China and caused hundreds of millions of rural Chinese to fall sick. Xi's new pollution-reducing policies benefited the whole country.

The world has criticized China for its mind-numbing levels of pollution, but if one looks deeper into the mirk, it becomes obvious that the worst violators were actually not mainlanders themselves but foreign businessmen like Mr. Lee taking advantage of China's economic desperation. As soon as jobs and food became more plentiful, the Chinese started to demand environmental protections.

In 2012, my firm, the China Market Research Group (CMR), interviewed 500 parents about their underlying concerns when buying products. Pollution and product quality remained their biggest concerns. They worried about buying toys or furniture made with toxic glue, so they often bought from brand-name companies like Lego and Ikea that they trusted not to use low-quality, toxic materials. They ate at KFC because they considered it "healthy"—it might be fried fast food, but they trusted that KFC would use good-quality ingredients.

Our surveys at CMR also indicated rising anger and concern among the population about their children's quality of life due to being raised in such a polluted and toxic environment. China suffered 400,000 premature deaths annually, blamed on high pollution levels. Parents were furious that factory owners, often exporting products to America and Europe, grew wealthy by literally poisoning the Chinese population.

Before Xi's crackdown on pollution, I almost moved out of China because I was worried about its effects on my family and their health. We did not want our son, Tom, exercising or even walking outdoors. We had him quit soccer because we wanted to limit his time outside and switch to indoor sports like basketball and squash. I used to carry him in my arms when taking him to school so that he didn't have to breathe in more of black air than he had to. We used to wrap his whole body from top to bottom so you could only see his eyes as we did not want any grit to touch his skin, potentially poisoning him. He looked like Boba Fett in *Star Wars*.

Consumers wealthy enough bought air purifiers and started to eat more healthily to counterbalance the effects of pollution. Sales of blueberries, Manuka honey and health supplements from companies like Blackmores or Swisse soared as consumers worried the toxicity of the air would harm them.

Chinese took vacations overseas to breathe in fresh air. Some 180 million Chinese traveled abroad every year before China shut its borders because of Covid, becoming the largest consumer spending group for many countries, including Thailand.

Vacationing overseas was not just about buying Gucci or LV handbags at duty free shops—it was about seeing natural beauty and experiencing nature. It was about taking a break from the pollution engulfing the country.

As Chinese traveled and saw how clean other countries were, many thought it was shameful that China's environment had become so degraded in the country's rush for money and economic growth. They started to complain online. Many wealthy people bought second or third homes in Sydney, Australia, or Irvine, California, where the air was cleaner. As one Chinese mother of two kids under the age of six told me, "I bought a home in Irvine because the quality of life and air are so good. I moved back to China for my children's early education so that my kids could learn Mandarin, but we will move back to Irvine as soon as their Mandarin is good enough." Many Chinese did not vocalize their frustrations—Chinese in general criticize the government publicly less than Americans—but they expressed their displeasure by emigrating to other countries, sending their kids to study abroad, or vacationing outside of China. Americans protest; Chinese immigrate.

If the 21st century is supposed to belong to China, shouldn't the country have clean air? many Chinese reasoned. How could China become a superpower if people were afraid to walk outside or eat fruits and vegetables grown in its soils? Pollution became a part of the national discourse with people checking the Air Quality Index on apps on a daily basis.

Xi and the government knew they had to do something and stop pollution, just as they had tackled corruption, even if it meant risking economic growth in the short term. They shut down factories belching black smoke and sediment into the air like Mr. Lee's. In Guangdong Province, the government developed a ten-year plan to replace low-end manufacturing like Acme Metal Fasteners with a mix of high-end manufacturing and innovative start-ups. It worked: Guangdong Province became a hub of innovation and advanced manufacturing, hosting companies like Huawei, DJI, and Tencent while Acme relocated to Vietnam

Despite losing factories like those of Mr. Lee's to countries like Vietnam and Sri Lanka, Jiangsu has become one of China's wealthiest provinces by cultivating a mix of tourism, the service sector, and high-end manufacturing. Mercedes has opened sprawling operations in the province. Hyatt opened the dazzling Park Hyatt Suzhou on the shores of Lake Jinji in the middle of an industrial park set up by the Singaporean government.

The pollution-reducing policies worked. Factories across China are now some of the cleanest in the world with zero-carbon emissions. Volkswagen and Airbus, for example, have built up some of their most advanced multibillion-dollar factories in the world in China, adhering to the strictest environment standards. I visited Volkswagen's Qingdao operations with my son Tom. The factory floor was as clean as the headquarters of an investment bank! The VW executives

touring me around told me how critical environmental protection was to their planning of operations. "We must adhere
to the highest standards of environmental protection," a senior Volkswagen employee told me.

Today, there are more clean air days than bad ones all over
China. In 2021, there were 288 sunny days in Beijing, compared to only 112 in 2013.[3] Today, you can hear the sound of
children playing in parks, while hiking and outdoor running
have become major hobbies for the fitness inclined as air pollution dissipates. The Beijing and Shanghai Marathons both
attract tens of thousands of participants.

China's newfound clean air has changed consumer habits. Using China's unparalleled infrastructure, tourists now
travel to areas of natural beauty within China like Yunnan,
Hainan and Xinjiang instead of going overseas to Bali and
Thailand. As they explore China's rugged terrain, they spend
more money on outdoor sports equipment and apparel
from jackets from Canada Goose to Salomon hiking shoes.
Hunan's Zhangjiajie, where the James Cameron movie *Avatar*
was filmed, has become famous for hosting extreme outdoor
sports along the mountain peaks. The popularity of rugged,
outdoor spots as well as marathons has soared across the
country.

Finding new growth drivers: NEVs and renewable energy

Aside from cracking down on high-polluting factories, to
go low carbon the government supported the adoption of
NEVs, wind power and photovoltaic products. City governments replaced gasoline-powered buses and taxi fleets with
NEVs. Local governments also pushed for consumers to
adopt NEVs through subsidies and by making it easy and

cheap to secure a license plate for a NEV vehicle while making it difficult and expensive to get a license plate for combustible engine cars.

Pushing NEVs has reduced pollution and allowed China to take the global lead in NEV technology. No foreign manufacturer can compete with the innovation coming from China's NEV sector through companies like Li Xiang, Xpeng, NIO, and BYD. Chinese NEVs are taking away share from legacy auto makers such as Toyota, Volkswagen, and Ford that have been slow to push for the adoption of NEVs. Unburdened by unions and internal power struggles from engineers and executives whose entire expertise relies on the internal combustible engine, Chinese NEV firms will dominate globally if unhampered by protectionist policies in the form of tariffs and by anti-Chinese sentiment.

The legacy auto manufacturers are behind the curve and have been too slow to adopt NEV technology. As one senior executive of a German auto manufacturer told me, "The Chinese electric vehicles are better than ours and cheaper. I understand why we have nearly a nonexistent market share in China in e-vehicles. We are in trouble if we do not evolve and adjust quickly enough and start producing and selling more competitive NEVs."

The government also undertook to reduce pollution by adopting renewable energy. They gave subsidies to the solar panel and wind turbine sectors to reduce the country's reliance on coal. Wind turbines dot the Chinese landscape. China has taken the lead in solar panel production in Xinjiang Province, which has become a hot point in US–China relations, as we saw previously. Combatting pollution has not only created healthier lifestyles, but also spurred new growth drivers like NEVs and clean energy.

Is China losing manufacturing competitiveness?

Whenever you hear about a large number of factories leaving China, China hawks say something along the lines of "This is because China is losing its competitiveness in manufacturing to other countries." This is simply not true. Low-end, high-polluting industries like Mr. Lee's are intentionally being pushed out of China by the government, as they simultaneously have limited economic benefits and cause too many environmental hazards. China no longer wants this kind of production—neither the jobs created by companies like Acme nor the pollution.

Even before Trump's and Biden's trade wars, countries that have lower environmental standards like Vietnam, Ethiopia, and India have gained market share for low-end light industry manufacturing. Acme has relocated much of its sourcing away from China and into Vietnam. Like China when it entered the WTO, countries in this region are desperate for foreign direct investment for job creation purposes. They are so poor they are willing to sacrifice air quality in order to create jobs.

The shift in light-end manufacturing toward Southeast Asia and other regions indicates China's antipollution policies are working, not that China is losing its manufacturing competitiveness. In fact, China continues to gain more high-end manufacturing such as the aerospace industry, associated with less pollution.

Pollution was also a major impediment to the growth of China's domestic tourism sector. Chinese longed for the blue skies they saw in Bali or Thailand; this was not possible to find in China throughout the 2010s. However, Xi's crackdown on pollution has been so successful that a lot of formerly polluted areas have now become popular tourist destinations. For example, Anji used to be one of the poorest parts of Zhejiang Province and by the early 2000s was synonymous with industrial pollution—from dye works, paper mills, cement factories, and quarries. Today, however, Anji has become a major destination for tourism. People visit to enjoy the stunning scenery and the tea fields.

Moreover, as Chinese tourists shy away from going to the US and other locations over worries about geopolitical tension and violence, more will be traveling within China to domestic hotspots like Yunnan, Hainan, Tibet, and Xinjiang in the post-Covid era.

Resolving water and soil pollution

When it comes to pollution, the next major challenge facing Xi is resolving water and soil pollution, both of which are harder to fix than air pollution but which may provide opportunities for foreign businesses to help with the effort. The US went through similar programs during the 1970s. When I was a schoolchild in New Hampshire, you could see foam bubbles when we swam in local rivers near my home in Concord, and we were told we could canoe but to be careful about jumping into the river because the water was so polluted. Now, it is common to canoe and swim safely in these same rivers.

China over the next several decades will continue tackling water and soil pollution, providing opportunities in the clean technology space. It is not a small issue which can be cleared up quickly: heavy industry factories from the 1970s to 2010s belched all sorts of waste into the air that seeped into the water and soil. Other factories ran off pollution directly into water supplies and the ground.

The soil pollution won't be easy to fix. For example, when I met with the Disney Imagineering team during the phased initial development and opening of Shanghai Disney, one of the senior executives said that the resources, time, and money required to clean the site's soil were a lot higher than originally envisioned. The senior executive told me: "The soil was just so much more contaminated than we expected. To make the soil safe for our guests, we had to spend a lot more time, money and effort processing the sand and bringing in other sand to make the area cleaner than we ever expected. The pollution reduction process added months, if not years, to the opening of Shanghai Disney."

Problems emerging from pollution have hit company after company, in addition to directly affecting Chinese consumers. Disney was hit with higher costs and production time overruns. Many companies have lost market share because consumers have worried soil pollution would hurt the quality of products. Most foreign brands like Enfamil and Similac import dairy from countries like Australia, the Netherlands, or New Zealand and only package in China as they knew Chinese parents were worried about quality control of the dairy system after the melamine scandals of 2008, when domestic baby formula producer Sanlu had its products adulterated with melamine, causing kidney problems for those who consumed the products: 296,000 children got sick; 52,898 were hospitalized.[4]

Nestlé tried to show respect for the Chinese government and people by saying its entire dairy supply chain was in China. This localization strategy backfired, however, as consumers were scared about the quality control. As one mother told me, "Even if I trust Nestlé and I trust the farmers that oversee the cows in Dongbei, I'm worried that the soil on which the grass to feed the cows is grown is contaminated from the heavily polluted soil." She went on: "This area [Northeast China] was a heavy industry area in the 1970s and 1980s, and the entire region is still famous for auto production." Nestlé always had a fairly lower market share in baby formula in China until it bought the Wyeth brand from Pfizer. Wyeth had a different supply chain from Nestlé's and thus was more trusted by Chinese mothers.

Over the last ten years, China has made remarkable strides in protecting the environment. From when I seriously considered relocating my family because of how bad the air pollution was to now when you can regularly see the blue sky in downtown Shanghai, the government has taken remarkable steps to improve the environment. They forced entire supply chains to either leave or install environmentally friendly manufacturing components that protected wildlife and ecology. Over the next ten to 20 years, environmental, social and governance (ESG) will continue to be a major theme related to China's economy.

The drive to reduce pollution is creating great opportunities for investments into clean technology fields and renewable energy. Reduced pollution will also create opportunities for companies working in areas that benefit from reduced pollution—for example the popularity of running and other outdoor activities is soaring, as is domestic Chinese tourism. And finally, the shifts in supply chains to countries like Vietnam will help create the rise of a middle class there too, even if such manufacturing for now is high polluting. Companies that benefited from China's early years of reform will see similar opportunities in fostering housing, education, and infrastructure in Vietnam, India, and other emerging manufacturing hubs.

Notes

1. Staff Writers, "China: 5,535 Students Died in '08 Earthquake," *NBC News*, May 7, 2009, https://www.nbcnews.com/id/wbna30611523

2. Yuwen Wu, "Profile: China's Fallen Security Chief Zhou Yongkang," *BBC News*, October 12, 2015, China https://www.bbc.com/news/world-asia-china-26349305

3. Staff Writers, "China's Air Becomes Cleaner Now, as Carbon Dioxide Emissions Per Unit of GDP Fall by Half from 2005," *Global Times*, June 18, 2022, https://www.globaltimes.cn/page/202206/1268427.shtml

4. China Daily, "Compensation work for tainted milk victims concluded," *China Daily*, March 2, 2009, https://www.chinadaily.com.cn/china/2009-03/02/content_7529731.htm

CHAPTER 11

Healthcare Reforms

Unlocking Middle-Class Spending

Aside from reducing pollution and corruption, one key area the Chinese government needed to address to maintain popular support among the 90 percent by the middle of the 2010s was making health care more accessible. Without access to health insurance or other social safety nets, Chinese families in the 90 percent saved for rainy days, as many remained one illness away from going bankrupt. The lack of a social safety net and rising health care costs is one reason why the savings rates (proportion of income set aside as savings) went from 33.59 percent in 1992 at the start of China's economic resurgence to 37.10 percent in 2015, before the government under Xi started to push for a more robust social safety net based on estimates by my firm CMR.[1] Aside from the Covid years which caused the figure to drop, US savings rates typically hover between 10 percent and 15 percent. The Chinese government realized to unlock consumption of both the 90 percent and the 10 percent it needed to reform its health care and insurance system to help shift the economy from the old growth playbook based on heavy investment and exports to one based on new growth drivers like consumption and services.

Without adequate insurance, Chinese families pool money from friends and family if someone gets sick. As one 28-year-old from Anhui working 15-hour days in a massage parlor lamented to me, "I remit nearly all my earnings back to my family to cover my father's medical expenses as he is very sick. I do not have much money left for myself to buy nice clothes or dine out with friends, but it is okay because it is for my father. I love him and have a duty to take care of him."

Previously, regulations forced companies to offer health insurance to workers but were typically only enforced in large companies and for white-collar workers. Employers in SMEs often never offered health insurance or any form of social security—workers often accepted illegal payment terms because it was hard in those days to get a decent job. Officials often enforced regulations loosely at the turn of the millennium especially in lower-tier cities where executives had good connections or could bribe officials. Authorities in poorer regions often cared more about receiving profit tax from corporations and creating jobs than ensuring companies paid for health coverage for the 90 percent. Top-line growth was a key KPI for promotions and tax revenue enabled local governments to spend freely on themselves in restaurants and health clubs—until Xi's crackdown on corruption.

One investment banker told me until 2008 she used to write in IPO prospectuses that one of the major risks to a company's profitability investors needed to be aware of was whether or not the government would enforce payment of health care and social security for all employees. "Local officials in provinces like Henan looked the other way in order to help companies go public to jumpstart the local economy and create jobs. Companies often created jobs in regions where enforcement of paying health coverage was lax so officials often turned a blind eye to companies that did not adhere to government regulations. But there is a risk that one day officials would crack down on companies that do not pay social security benefits. Investors need to be aware of that." In the early years of China's accession to the WTO, job creation and filling the state coffers with tax money remained the most pressing concern. Companies often paid off corrupt local officials to look the other way when breaking labor laws, too. A wad of cash or an ATM debit card with an accompanying password was all it took for officials to overlook labor law abuses.

Many in the 90 percent working in sectors like hospitality or hair and beauty as well as streetside vendors and sole entrepreneurs selling products on Taobao do not get fixed salaries. They get paid based 100 percent on commission and never receive health insurance coverage. The lack of a stable or minimum salary is one reason why consumer spending has remained low in the post-Covid era—tens of millions of Chinese earned literally nothing when zero-Covid policies shut down entire cities for months at a time, locking down 300 million Chinese at one point.

Workers in commission-based jobs often change employment and even cities and provinces every few months as they seek higher salaries or try seeking their fortunes in different regions. For them, receiving or paying into a local health insurance based on city of employment is impossible or undesirable, so they take compensation upfront in cash as much as possible and save their wages in case their families face a rainy day. China needs to install a unified system where workers can get medical coverage no matter what city or province they are in, or where they can transfer coverage easily, rather than it being based solely on where they work. As one retired 63-year-old women originally from Jiangsu, Mrs. Wang, told me, "I worked in Beijing my whole life and fortunately have earned medical care coverage here. I would like to spend more time with my daughter who lives in Shanghai, but I am not sure my insurance covers there, so I do not spend as much time as I would like visiting family just in case I get sick while there. I do not want to be out of pocket to see a doctor in Shanghai."

Retired workers, many of them former farmers, have often never worked in a company that offered insurance, so, as they grow older, they have to rely on younger generations to help pay medical bills. Before the one-child policy (1979–2015), many farmers would have as many children as possible, hopefully boys, as a form of health insurance. With retirees in the 2010s becoming the first generation to grow old with only one child to support them, the financial burden on families, especially the young generation, has become too high.

To address access to health challenges, by the late 2010s the government began to enforce *yibao* and other insurance coverage laws and to make it easier for patients to use insurance in cities outside of their place of employment. Employees could take their employers to court if they did not provide them with a social insurance program such as *shebao*. Instead of looking the other way, Xi's crackdown on corruption ensured officials enforced judgments and penalized companies that were bad actors. Sustainable and high-quality economic growth—especially nonpolluting growth—became key KPIs for officials looking to get promoted.

Private enterprises also began to sell insurance that made it possible for people to buy into health insurance plans, and this has led to private hospitals sprouting up all over the country. The sale of private insurance plans by companies like Ping An, China Life, and foreign insurance providers like Allianz and AXA soared as increasingly wealthy consumers wanted to seek treatment at private hospitals in China and, for more serious cases, internationally. Often set up to target foreign expatriates, foreign-invested hospitals like United and Parkway soon found that a significant chunk, if not the majority, of their client base were wealthy Chinese. Private insurance offered better coverage and flexibility in hospital choice than state insurance plans.

Tech giants like Ant Financial also started to offer various forms of insurance, and it was common for travel sites like Ctrip to add various forms of health and evacuation insurance when people bought plane tickets. These companies made it easy to buy insurance via apps. What used to be a time-consuming process of going to an insurance agent's office and signing a mound of paperwork quickly became accessible to Chinese with a click of a button and payment online via WeChat Pay or Alipay. For the first time in the history of China, the majority of the 90 percent has some sort of health insurance, often the government-mandated scheme plus supplementary coverage through the private sector.

For some illnesses and medicines, the government coverage is 100 percent; for others there are copayments, but the burden is heavily reduced. Having insurance has reduced anxiety for consumers and unlocked spending money for discretionary purchases like holidays, dining out, and apparel. Household savings rates dropped from 2016 to 2019 before they went up again due to consumer worries about the US–China trade war and Covid. The Peterson Institute found that, through the first half of 2023, Chinese household saving rates went up by 15 percent year on year, up to 12 trillion yuan from 7.5 trillion yuan in January 2019.[2] But the long-term trend is clear—reforms in the insurance and health care system will unleash spending for the 90 percent.

Giving the 90 percent health care access and building political support

Having access to health care to even previously forgotten workers has made the 90 percent loyal to the ruling CPC. Xi Jinping himself has taken on a cult-like status in regions like Tibet, in a way that no other CPC leader has had, aside from Mao Zedong himself. Xi is seen as shepherding health care access to every Chinese household. These workers form the bedrock of support for the CPC despite the flagging economy.

Getting access to health care coverage for the first time in Chinese history is why the 90 percent of the country hold Xi Jinping and the ruling CPC in such high esteem—in the last ten years there has been material improvements to the quality of their lives, much as citizens in Tier 1 cities saw such an increase in their living standards after China acceded to the WTO. Despite the flagging economy in the post-Covid era, support for the CPC is at an all-time high in the poorer regions whose populations are now able to get access to medical care and education. This contrasts with rising pessimism among the 10 percent and those living in Tier 1 cities. Unlike the elite, the 90 percent do not care as much about the concentration of power that often slows decision-making—they just want a ruling party that is stable and helps them improve the lives of their families.

Although the improvements in access to health care access are undeniable, China's health care system, is plagued by a lack of properly trained doctors, creating opportunities for foreign businesses to grow as China continues to reform the system. Better doctors gravitate toward Tier 1 and Tier 2 cities like Beijing and Hangzhou where salaries are higher. Doctors left practicing in rural areas are not as well trained as their big-city counterparts and do not have access to the same equipment and resources.

Under the Jiang Zemin and Hu Jintao administrations, the government focused on building large, flagship hospitals in large cities that were as well equipped as famous hospitals in the US and Europe like Cedars-Sinai Medical Center in Los Angeles or the Dana Farber Cancer Institute in Boston. The Ministry of Health encouraged these flagship hospitals to buy medical equipment from Western brands like Siemens and GE to prove that China was catching up to the West in health care capabilities. When entering these flagship hospitals, patients found the equipment and hygiene standards rivaled top institutions in the US.

Chinese hospitals also sent doctors overseas to the Mayo Clinic, MGH, Johns Hopkins, and other top hospital chains for training and to forge prestige relations. Doctors returned well trained and equipped to handle severe illnesses. I have had three surgeries while in China—all my surgeons trained and practiced in the US. However, the numbers of doctors who have trained and practiced abroad are limited and tend to practice in Tier 1 cities in China after returning home, adding to the inequality in health provision between wealthy urban elite and poorer populations in lower-tier cities.

Fears of poor-quality health care in rural areas caused peasants to trek to larger cities to seek health care access in provincial capitals and Tier 1 cities, even for minor ailments. Famous hospitals like Shanghai's Huashan or Ruijin Hospitals became swamped with patients. Doctors in flagship hospitals could see as many as 100–200 patients a day while doctors in less famous hospitals would only see a few patients.

By the second half of the Hu Jintao administration (2007–12), the government began to address the problems of crowding and inefficient allocation of resources and started to de-emphasize flagship hospitals. The government started funneling money to establish neighborhood health care facilities and to improve rural hospitals. Hospitals bought cheaper equipment, mostly from domestic medical device companies like Mindray. The government also started to concentrate on buying pharmaceuticals at the provincial or national level rather than at individual hospitals.

Marketing campaigns emphasized that community hospitals were cheap and good enough and convenient for treating most ailments, and that there was no need to travel to far-off hospitals in big cities for every single illness.

The government also started to rotate doctors from Tier 1 cities who were Communist Party members to spend three-year stints in the countryside to help uplift the quality of health care in these regions. These doctors brought a wealth of knowledge to local areas. The government also sent doctors in rural areas to train in Tier 1 cities as well. I hurt my foot, for instance while playing soccer in Mulei, Xinjiang. The doctor who treated me had trained for several years in Jishuitan Hospital in Beijing, perhaps China's most famous hospital for orthopedics.

A doctor's visit at 4000 meters up

I felt my knees starting to wobble. I had just finished lunch in a restaurant in a small Tibetan village and was walking toward the car. I felt dizzy, and then, suddenly, my legs gave out and I collapsed to the ground. My friend grabbed me, carried me to a car, and screamed, "Get him to a hospital!"

The pain in my head was intense. It felt like someone had taken a sledgehammer to the right side of my head. I was shaking all over—I am not sure whether this was due to the fever that was overwhelming my body or just my fear. When we had arrived in Tibet, the hotel manager told me several tourists died every year because they could not handle the high altitude.

The driver rushed me to a desolate village hospital 4000 meters above sea level. Nurses pulled me into a hospital room and put an IV into me. My blood oxygen level was only 60 percent of a normal reading. The doctor, a thin, short man, came over to me and said, "Don't worry. You are safe. We are going to take care of you."

As he was speaking, my friend asked, "Are you from Shandong Province?"

The doctor smiled and said, "Yes, I am!"

It turned out that my friend and the doctor were originally from districts just miles away from each other in Jinan, the capital of Shandong Province. After my fever went down, I asked the doctor about his life story. He was a Communist Party member who had been sent to this remote village for a three-year posting to train local doctors to help improve health care quality.

Critics of the CPC do not realize how much Party members must sacrifice for the Party and thus the country to remain in good standing. Too often Western media portrays Party members as power-hungry, corrupt individuals selfishly feathering their own beds. While corruption still exists, the reality is that many Party members like the doctor sacrifice themselves for the well-being of the country. They are sent to poor provinces for three-year durations, often away from their families, to carry out the country's reform initiatives.

My acupuncturist in Shanghai, for example, treats patients at the famous Shuguang Hospital, but he also has to treat patients in a community hospital every Tuesday to bring cheap, affordable health care to mostly older Chinese. When I see him at Shuguang, it costs thirty times more than the price he offers in the community hospitals. The care and expertise he offers is the same. The main difference is that there is a shorter waiting period in Shuguang but the care is the same.

To increase access to health care, the government bolsters community hospitals by sending doctors from Tier 1 hospitals to practice there and providing the hospitals with good-quality medical equipment and pharmaceuticals. Seeing famous doctors practice in neighborhood hospitals, patients begin to trust the quality of care there, which eases the crowding in Tier 1 hospitals. By relying upon doctors who are Party members, the Party can push forward health care reforms. Without these Party members, there is no way China could have reformed the rural health care so quickly—top talent normally would not choose to work in regions with such harsh conditions.

The CPC's carrot-and-stick approach to promotions makes the Chinese political system work. There are 96 million Party members who often sacrifice their home life to carry out the Party's health care and poverty alleviation policies in far-flung regions of China. They often have to put the needs of the Party and the country in front of the needs of their own family.

Back in my hospital room in Tibet, I could see that the system was working. The hospital itself was hygienic, clean, and well lit. They had top-notch equipment from European and Chinese medical device companies. This was so different from my experiences of hospital care 25 years previously when I had first arrived in China in 1997, when hospitals in Tianjin were physically falling apart, there was not enough equipment, and where I saw doctors reusing needles and smoking cigarettes while tending to patients.

Unlocking savings

One of the biggest barriers toward unlocking consumption in China is the lack of health insurance and a social safety net. While consumption accounts for 70 percent of America's economy, until recently in China it lagged behind at around 35 percent. Today, consumption accounts for 50 percent of the economy—according to estimates by my firm, China Market Research Group—but it still lags behind most developed countries. Many Chinese still save for a rainy day as they still do not fully trust the social security net offered by China. They have lived through too many ups and downs and political chaos to fully embrace government programs. They rely on themselves and their families just in case. As one 31-year-old blue-collar worker in Jiangsu Province told me, "My family saves enough money to take care of my parents in case they get sick when they are older and insurance does not cover them. Luckily, I am wealthy enough to get them a helper if need be."

Saving for a rainy day will continue until the masses see social programs working for decades and policies remaining stable. The government recognizes that, to alleviate worries and spur consumption, it will need to demonstrate that better access to health care is here to stay. The government has done four things:

1. It has forced employers, even in formerly grey employment areas, to pay into the state *yibao* insurance program.

2. It has made it easier for people from different provinces to get reimbursed when they seek medical care in other provinces.

3. It has kept the price of medical appointments, especially in community hospitals, capping medicine prices and rolling out private insurance.

4. It has built hospitals in rural areas and forced doctors from Tier 1 cities to staff these hospitals, in order to provide better access to patients and train local doctors.

These four actions will all significantly impact consumer spending among the 90 percent and create opportunities for companies in the health care sector.

A visit to a hospital in Xinjiang for Uyghurs

"I think I'm going cry," I said to my friend Emily. We had just entered a rehabilitation hospital for children born with physical and mental disabilities in Kashgar, Xinjiang. In front of me, lying on the floor, were almost two dozen children under the age of six who could not walk, many of whom also had mental disabilities. My heart broke as I saw forlorn parents hugging their children, but I recovered slightly when I saw that each child was also being cared for by a team of physical therapists and nurses dedicated to improving the children's lives.

In this Kashgar children's rehabilitation hospital I visited, over 90 percent of families and patients were Uyghur, with treatment completely free of charge for all from Kashgar between the ages of several months to six years old. The hospital also provided funding for patients and their families to live in the hospital for free ten months a year. Funding for this endeavor is provided by the Disabled Providence Fund, which companies across the country (like mine in Shanghai) pay into every month. It was nice to visibly see the taxes I paid as a small business owner making a difference to the lives of these children. While I was there, I witnessed not only physical therapy but also a singing class; these children were being educated, too. The head of the hospital was a Han Chinese who told me that he had set up the program to create a better quality of life for Uyghurs. All of the hospital's funding comes from the government. Almost all the therapists and nurses— as well as patients—were Uyghur.

I interviewed one Uyghur mother whose daughter was four years old. She said she was thankful for the hospital. Previously, she had had pay for her child's care out of her own pocket at a run-down hospital near her home. Now, because the Chinese government offered free treatment and housing, she had seen her child begin to speak and improve her walking abilities. Staff are optimistic that the woman's daughter will be able to join regular school classes with other children in the next two to three years. When I left the hospital ward that day, her daughter beamed at me and said, "Khosh"— "goodbye" in Uyghur.

The Chinese government collects funds from wealthier provinces predominantly populated by Han Chinese and allocates them to poorer provinces. Funds from Shanghai were used to support Kashgar. The hospital provided support to Uyghur children with mental and physical disabilities, rather than consigning them to a life of little opportunity, helping with their rehabilitation journeys to allow them more connection with society as a whole. This is very different than how the Western media portrays policies in Xinjiang.

Not only is health care coverage improving the lives of the Uyghurs I met, but the coverage is also unlocking savings. Uyghurs feel their new insurance coverage means they did not need to save so much of their earnings for a rainy day. Uyghurs thus spent more on clothes, shoes, food, and other daily necessities. They are like the 42-year-old party secretary in Tibet who told me that access to health care was one of the reasons (aside from infrastructure) that he and his family were now so optimistic about their futures. With the government providing insurance covering about 80 percent of medical care, Tibetan and Uyghur villagers only have to cover the remaining 20 percent.

Encouraging births

In a village outside Yili, Xinjiang, I met a Uyghur family the day they brought their baby girl—their third child—home from the hospital. Although it ended almost a decade ago, many do not realize that China's one-child policy focused on restricting birthrates for Han Chinese—minorities like Uyghurs were allowed to have two or three children depending on their location.[3] This Uyghur family already had two boys, aged 10 and 12. The mother told me she had always wanted a daughter, so they tried for years to have one.

The father told me that both of his sons had been born in a simple, unsanitary village room. They had had to spend around 1000 RMB per birth for his two sons. When their daughter was born, it had been at a newly built hospital that was as large and clean as any hospital in China. State insurance covered almost the entire cost of the birth. The father told me he only paid around 200 RMB (around 30 USD) for the birth of their daughter. The mother was so happy, not only because she had a baby girl but also because she was able to give birth in a clean, well-staffed hospital at a fraction of the cost of the birth of her sons ten-plus years before.

Improving access to health care has spread throughout China, even to poorer regions like Xinjiang. More, though, needs to be done despite the reforms. Hospitals remain overcrowded and lack ICU beds. China only has 3.6 ICU beds per 100,000 people while the US has 34.2, Italy 12.5, and Germany 29.2.[4] The lack of ICU beds is one of the reasons why China was so scared about opening up and living with Covid—it worried it did not have enough ICU beds to treat people when Covid ripped through the population.

The number of hospitals and doctors per capita is also too low. China has just one physician per 6666 people, versus the international standard of one doctor for every 1500–2000 people. Unlike in America, salaries for doctors in China remain low. While doctors in the US are typically considered part of the upper class, in China doctors are in the middle class. In 2015, the average physician's salary was only 13,764 USD.

The demand for continued heath care reform provides opportunities for investment by the private sector. However, investors must not forget about the Common Prosperity initiative. They cannot invest in the health care sector that benefits the 10 percent only, or in a way that takes advantage of the 90 percent, as the risks of a crackdown like the one we saw in the education sector remain high.

During the Hu Jintao years, the government encouraged the setting up of private hospitals and allowed public hospitals to offer VIP service. Both charged market rates that targeted the 10 percent. However, under Xi, the VIP services in public hospitals have had prices capped and the service offerings reduced—in the new China, there cannot be a two-tiered system for the haves and have-nots in public hospitals. Originally set up to cater to expatriate families, private hospital chains like Parkway and United are shifting their target markets away from expatriates to upper-middle-class Chinese. They have cut prices in half to attract more volume at the expense of margins.

Reforms in the health care sector will continue, leaving opportunities for pharmaceutical and medical device companies. However, profits will be capped because the government views health care access as a cornerstone of reducing income inequality as part of Xi's overall Common Prosperity drive. The government will simply not allow health care companies to profit too much, just like it did not let education sector entrepreneurs profit too much.

Companies need to be aware that, while there is the potential for huge profits in the medical sector, the sector is ultimately viewed as a public good. Profits will come from volume rather than through fat margins, and ultimately companies in the sector will have to deal with heavy regulation.

Improving health care access for all Chinese is essentially an extension of China's Common Prosperity initiative. Yet while profit margins will be capped in order to ensure access to medicine and medical equipment, there is still enormous opportunity in the health care sector. Eight hundred and fifty million more people are going to get access to health care and good medical care and equipment over the next 20 years. Such reforms will create significant opportunity from a volume perspective for health care companies. Giving Chinese access to health care will also unlock consumer spending and give rise to a vibrant middle class, which will give profit opportunities in other sectors such as sports apparel, tourism, and cosmetics.

Notes

1. OECD database on Trading Economics, last accessed May 14, 2024, https://tradingeconomics.com/china/personal-savings#:~:text=Personal%20Savings%20in%20China%20averaged,of%2027.20%20percent%20in%202002

2. Tianlei Huang and Mary E. Lovely, "Half a Year Into China's Reopening after Covid, Private Economic Activity Remains Weak," *PIIE*, July 31, 2023, https://www.piie.com/blogs/realtime-

economics/half-year-chinas-reopening-after-Covid-private-economic-activity-remains

3. https://lkyspp.nus.edu.sg/gia/article/what-did-china's-one-child-policy-mean-for-minorities

4. "ICU Beds per Capita by Country 2024," *World Population Review*, https://worldpopulationreview.com/country-rankings/icu-beds-per-capita-by-country

CHAPTER 12

Income Inequality

The Rise of the Fuerdai

Foreign businesspeople joked in the early 2000s they loved doing business in Red China because it was the most capitalistic nation on earth. China was a heaven for people who believed in Reaganomics and trickle-down theory—under Prime Minister Zhu Rongji during the Jiang Zemin era, the State ended the Iron Rice Bowl of lifetime employment to push for a market-oriented economy and deregulated industries. Health care was paid on a pay-as-you-go basis; there were no inheritance or annual real estate taxes, and entrepreneurs could buy homes, Bentleys, and even massage parlor memberships and write them off as business expenses. China became heaven for "master of the universe" types. And with charities all run by the State, the wealthy did not even feel that it was expected for them to give back to society through charity work—helping poor people was the job of the government.

By the late 1990s, the reforms spurred go-go growth with the economy soaring at a 10 percent clip annually as the government pursued top-line economic growth at all costs. After decades of being anticapitalist, the central government needed to demonstrate to local cadres that private business and profits were acceptable. Officials had growth metrics placed as part of their KPIs for promotion. It did not matter if the growth caused pollution or income inequality—all that mattered was top-line growth.

During these heady days, many provinces saw annual growth top 15 percent. The rich got richer as they used connections to secure contracts with state-owned enterprises (SOEs). The best connected, often the sons and daughters of senior officials, simply took over SOEs at cut-rate prices. All one needed to get wealthy was close connections with Party officials or the willingness to bribe. As one man who was married to the daughter of a senior official told me, "I got monopolistic rights selling Australian wine to one ministry. What a deal! I make so much money."

Corrupt officials and well-connected businesspeople fueled the sales of luxury goods from Louis Vuitton to Chanel and luxury homes. Businesspeople gave diamond-encrusted Omega watches to officials to secure deals and protection.

Real estate prices soared. Before limits on the number of houses one could buy were implemented, those well connected enough to get bank loans between 2003 and 2008 could buy as many homes as they wanted with little or no down payment. A friend who was a partner in a Big Four accounting firm bought six apartments at 250,000–500,000 USD each that are now worth 5–10 million USD each. Those with access to bank loans bought several hundred apartments with zero percent down. Within a few years, they had net worths of several hundred million USD. The founders of some well-known Chinese companies told me they made more money from buying hundreds of apartments than in their own business—even ones they took public for billions of dollars.

Wealthy insiders and those rich from real estate or taking over SOEs began to consume, creating whole new industries, from travel to tourism to clothing. FDI flowed into China from the whole world as every businessman or woman and investor wanted a piece of the China Dream.

Senior executives used SOEs as personal piggybanks and took bribes. One restaurateur in Beijing in 2004 told me, "The average ticket price to eat in my restaurant for four people is 3200 USD." Almost all of his clients were government officials and executives from SOEs using tax dollars to live like billionaires. SOE executives cared about enriching themselves, not about making corporate profits. As one senior banker told me in 2007, "I care about lending money to other state-owned enterprises; I don't really care about retail customers and their needs."

Risk-taking entrepreneurs like Alibaba's Jack Ma helped resolve inefficiencies in the economy, making the markets more competitive and innovative. The positive impact private entrepreneurs like Ma had on Chinese society should not be underestimated. He created payment systems like Alipay because banks were too slow to issue credit cards. Banks did not have the knowledge or the data to build up credit bureaus outside of the largest cities nor did they care about retail customers. In 2005, there were only 13.5 million credit cards in circulation as the state-owned banks spent little time and effort on building up their consumer retail business—bank bosses got promoted by doling out loans to state-owned banks. They did not care about everyday retail customers.

The private sector also helped the government streamline services that SOEs should have done—from paying electricity bills and speeding fines to booking hospital visits via apps. The positive effects Jack Ma had on reforming inefficiencies in the economy should not be understated—he solved so many issues for society.

Deregulation (and, truth be told, corruption in some cases) jumpstarted the economy and incentivized risk taking. Corruption by definition is wrong, but in the 1990s some corruption benefited the economy as regulations were still stuck in the 1960s when private business was considered evil—corrupt officials greenlighted infrastructure and privatization plans that ultimately reformed and pushed the economy to new heights.

Downsides to the wealth creation of the go-go years emerged by the mid-2010s—corruption started to hurt the economy as it was so widespread, and—perhaps even more worryingly for China's economic planners—the wealth creation benefited the 10 percent at the expense of the 90 percent. The 90 percent saw their quality of life improve in a form of trickle-down economics—they could now eat meat and buy adidas gear—but the Gini co-efficient or income gap rose, causing anger at how unfair the system had become.

While lower- and middle-class Chinese were now able to put food on their tables they were relatively worse off compared with the 10 percent. In the early 2010s, the Communist Party saw its legitimacy tainted as many poor residents no longer viewed the Party as representing the masses but just themselves and the 10 percent.

The widening income gap was even more pronounced when geographical location was factored in—wealth was concentrated in Tier 1 cities like Shanghai, Beijing, and Shenzhen compared to impoverished provinces like Heilongjiang, Gansu, and Guizhou. Beijing's average GDP per capital in 2020 was 164,904 RMB while Gansu's was only 36,038 RMB.[1] The best universities like Tsinghua University, Peking University, and Shanghai Jiaotong University are all located in Tier 1 cities, too. It is easier for native residents of those cities to gain entry to these universities, further exacerbating the regional differences in opportunity. It would be like Boston residents having preferential access to gaining admittance into Harvard or MIT.

The rich got richer, while the poor got relatively poorer. Social discontent with the unfair advantages Tier 1 city residents had was rising. One's wealth and comfort in life were often based on where one was born—something that was clearly unfair.

Wanting to rejuvenate the CPC and to create a more equitable, socialist society, Xi revived the Common Prosperity initiative, which had originated under Mao Zedong but had not been in operation for decades. Common Prosperity became the bedrock of Xi's drive to tackle income disparity. His plan has been to help the 90 percent gain more equal opportunities and a fairer share of the economy, even if that meant demoralizing the 10 percent. By creating more equitable opportunities, Xi also re-legitimized the CPC, with the masses once again believing the Party is looking out after the interests of the "little guy," not just the rich and well connected.

Dining at the top of the world

Pierre pointed to a sparkling crystal chandelier hanging from the ceiling and said, "It's stunning, isn't it? I don't know how much it costs, but maybe several hundred thousand dollars if they are Baccarat chandeliers."

We were dining in a private room on the 90th story of the J Hotel, the world's highest hotel, located in the heart of Shanghai's Lujiazui financial district, where the price per head for dinner often goes north of 1000 USD. Pierre and I were talking about areas of business cooperation. In my mind, I gave Pierre the nickname "Pierre the Man Child," even though he was in his late thirties, because of his profligate spending and hard partying. He had three children from three different women across different continents. The Man Child collected cars like Rolls-Royces or Bentleys like Chinese schoolchildren collect Ultraman cards. He once lost 20 million USD on a single alcohol-and-hooker-fueled trip to Las Vegas. Pierre was the sole heir to a sprawling empire.

As soon as I met Pierre, I liked "The Man Child" but was shocked at how easily he spent his father's money... He was generous—I saw him give out multi-thousand-dollar gifts of jewelry to friends and hangers-on without a second thought.

The Man Child told me that he had not left the hotel in five days. He laughed: "I eat every meal in the Hotel." He was as comfortable in a Chinese setting as in a Western one, as he had spent half of his life studying in the US before moving back to China to help run his father's empire.

Pierre epitomizes four issues stemming from wealth creation in China that Xi and the CPC are trying to address:

1. Excessive wealth is concentrated in the hands of 10 percent of the population while the masses (the 90 percent) struggle to pay for their children's education and family health care costs. Such a disparity is unacceptable in a socialist nation. All initiatives, from Common Prosperity to the education and training crackdown, need to be viewed through the lens of the CPC trying to reduce income inequality.

2. The shift in wealth creation in China from Tier 1 cities to Tier 3–5 cities in the late 2010s has created a newly embedded elite class in rural areas. This newfound class of the wealthy is concentrated in cities where there are few real estate purchase limits but which are fairly close to magnet cities like Shanghai. In these areas, the wealthy are

buying up 100–200 apartments, just like speculators did in Shanghai and Beijing during the 2003–8 Golden Period.

3. Spending power is switching from the older generations who made their wealth as entrepreneurs in the 1990s to their children who were born with silver spoons in their mouths. These children tend to be well educated and worldly but do not have the entrepreneurial drive of the first generation.

4. The wealthy are getting increasingly concerned that they will become the target of corruption crackdowns and new policies that will hurt their ability to make money. Many are semi-retiring and waiting until the political winds get warmer. Others are shifting capital offshore, so that they have backup money in case they need to flee China if the situation for rich people continues to deteriorate

In the 1980s through the 2010s, most wealth was created by insiders and entrepreneurs in China's Tier 1 cities like Beijing, Shanghai, and Shenzhen, which served as magnets for foreign direct investment. The government rolled out targeted tax and other benefits to foreign companies to invest in these magnet cities and pushed SOEs to set up headquarters and subsidiaries there.

Risk taking characterized the entrepreneurs of this era. They were typically not well connected by birth and had nothing to lose in venturing into risky new business deals or even by bribing their way to wealth. They had to succeed and cut corners or else their families wouldn't eat.

Starting in the 2010s, however, major wealth creation started to be generated from poorer regions due to benefits accrued from infrastructure construction and limits on buying real estate in Tier 1 cities. Multinational and domestic firms alike started moving investments toward the central and western parts of China. The government ordered SOEs to open more subsidiaries in these regions to boost local development. This shift toward economic growth in developing regions enabled Pierre's father to get obscenely rich—using his factories to generate cash flow to buy real estate on the cheap in dozens of cities around China before other rural residents were able to take out bank loans to buy homes. Pierre's father had bought hundreds of apartments all over China as well as commercial offices.

Tibetan villagers use newly built roads to attract tourists and sell peaches—Pierre's family uses infrastructure reforms to get dazzlingly rich. Aside from making his real estate investments more valuable, the new transportation systems let Pierre's father buy and sell commodities and use transportation links to get the products in and out of areas that just ten years prior would have been unreachable.

Pierre's family got obscenely rich—they flew private jets and hobnobbed with billionaires around the world, from Russian oligarchs to US billionaires.

As the children of wealthy entrepreneurs reached adult age, they started making more prominent spending decisions both in their personal lives and for their parent's companies. This was the case for Pierre. His spending habits have ramifications for the luxury ecosystem as well as the emergence of the private wealth sector and equity markets.

Pierre is from a city in Zhejiang Province that I had never heard of. His father, Mr. Wu, had made a fortune in real estate, commodities, and other ventures. As he got wealthier, he had invested in real estate in America.

Mr. Wu's son Pierre was the epitome of the *fuerdai*, or the second-generation wealthy: friendly, smart, and generous, but also hard partying, a little lazy, and spoiled beyond belief.

Pierre received a healthy allowance from his father and had no accountability for any of his spending or business ventures, which had often gone belly up, losing millions of dollars.

Pierre had never had to work a day in his life except within his father's conglomerate. As a result, he spent lavishly—on himself and on his friends. I could not tell whether he was doing so to buy friendship or because he was truly a generous person.

Pierre looked at me as he poured me a shot of Moutai, the famed burning liquor distilled from fermented sorghum that has become the main alcoholic drink served at Chinese state banquets and celebrations.

"This bottle is good," Pierre said, "and I know alcohol. This bottle is cheap—it's only 2000 or 3000 USD—but it's better than the real expensive Moutai I normally drink." I was astounded at the exorbitant amount Pierre spent on alcohol. Seemingly every time I met him, he had a bottle of Moutai or a *grand cru* or a 99-point graded bottle of red wine from California or France that ran to the hundreds of thousands of dollars a bottle.

"I like the aftertaste, even though it is cheap."

Although the government has targeted more even income distribution between Tier 1 and lower-tier cities, they are running into a new problem that will ultimately need to be resolved—wealth is again being concentrated in lower-tier cities by families like Pierre's. Unlike in Shanghai and other Tier 1 cities where, to stop prices from spiraling, there are now strict limits on the number of homes one can buy, many Tier 3 cities do not have limitations on the number of homes one can buy as the government is desperate to raise money via real estate sales. The result is wealthy locals are scooping up villas and apartments and benefiting from the price increases as the rural areas get better connected through infrastructure spending.

In these areas, wealth inequality is becoming more pronounced and is creating an ensconced wealthy class. Without inheritance tax and/or even annual real estate tax in most cities, the wealthy in these lower-tier cities just kept getting richer and richer while the poor have no chance. Ultimately, the government will have to move to reduce this inequality in rural areas in the same way it has in Tier 1 cities.

Spending on luxury

Originally from Shanghai, the 27-year-old Isabelle—"Princess"—had graduated from an Ivy League university with a Master's degree, and was married to a man who had barely graduated from a fifth-tier university in the US. Like Pierre, her husband worked for his father's business empire which was headquartered in a Tier 3 city in Jiangsu Province. They had a two-year-old son.

Decked out in Gucci shoes, a Celine handbag, and Bulgari earrings, the strikingly beautiful Isabelle told me about her favorite brands that she bought for herself and her son. She pointed to her very large Harry Winston engagement ring, explaining that nobody bought Tiffany's anymore—anybody who is anyone buys a Harry Winston diamond these days.

She had met her husband when both were studying in the US. Her husband's family were even wealthier than hers. Her in-laws had initially built their fortune around commodities trading. Thirty years ago, her husband's family were farmers. Her father-in-law ventured into buying scrap metal from other farmers and selling it to small factories. He eventually turned his one-man show into a giant conglomerate buying and selling lithium for batteries and investing in real estate. His mix of business acumen and risk taking has paid off. Today, Princess's father-in-law drives a bevy of luxury cars like Mercedes Maybach, a Range Rover, and a Ferrari and has hundreds of houses all over China, including a 2000-square-meter mansion in his hometown that looks like a European castle.

Princess was smart, funny, and, like Pierre, spoiled to death. Whatever Princess wanted, Princess's husband got her, with money given to him by his father. Whether it be a Ferrari or a Porsche or a new villa or a jaunt around the world, her husband pampered her with the best money could buy. They spent over 1 million USD on their wedding. Her biggest complaint in life is that her husband's hometown is boring. So she tries to visit Shanghai or Hong Kong whenever she has time; otherwise she feels stuck in the countryside.

There was only one salon near her home that offered Thermage®, a cosmetic procedure. This salon, Isabelle told me, actually charged double what a salon in Shanghai did, because there was so little competition. It was packed with many women, especially older women, who preferred to stay in their own city and were not as willing as younger folk to venture regularly to Shanghai. But they wanted only the best beautification products and services and were willing to spend extra to receive treatments from the "in place" that everyone who was anyone in their hometown visited.

Isabelle and her friends were still in their twenties so enjoyed trips to Shanghai to shop and party. Even though they were still wrinkle free, they purchased ultra-expensive luxury cosmetics because they considered them to be the best. They got permanent eyebrow tattoos and skin-tightening treatments. In other words, they were spending on the products and services that in America target wealthy forty-something women, and they were purchasing them for themselves with money given to them by their parents or parent-in-laws. Those with children decked them out in branded clothes, from JNBY to Burberry to Gucci. Like Pierre, they are unimaginably wealthy but have little accountability in their day-to-day work habits. "Many of the young people in my husband's hometown went to the United States and Canada to study," Isabelle said, "at second- and third-tier colleges, but few actually graduated, because there are so rich and life is so much easier back in China. Many dropped out of school to join their parent's company."

China's *fuerdai* like Princess and her family are a policy problem for China's government from a social stability standpoint. The control *fuerdai* hold over local economies especially in lower-tier cities is unfair. Because China does not have an inheritance tax and most smaller cities do not have an annual real estate tax or a limit on the number of homes one can purchase, these families are creating unimaginable wealth that will filter down the generations. They have bought scores of apartments and villas as a wealth preservation safety net in case their main businesses go under. Since they do not have to pay annual tax on these houses, they often go unrented.

Many of these families are only going to continue getting wealthier as they hold the rural or peasant *hukou*, which enables them to buy and build gigantic mansions on farmland in the middle of nowhere. Urban *hukou* holders are not allowed to buy homes on land registered as rural so often in this situation one family member keeps or applies for a rural *hukou* to enable the whole family to buy and build mansions.

Isabelle has one of these giant mansions that she does not like because it is too far away from lively shopping and dining areas. However, as China's infrastructure spending increases, farmland mansions which were once inconveniently remote are now becoming easily reachable from major cities, driving the prices of these mansions to tens of millions of dollars.

Her husband's hometown, for instance, now has a high-speed train stop on a route into Shanghai. The government is trying to create an area linked into the Shanghai Hongqiao airport system. As with the Tibetan villages, the outskirts of this city are now set to become a major beneficiary of China's infrastructure spending.

While this wealth creation is good for brands targeting the newly minted wealthy, the *fuerdai* also pose a major problem for Xi Jinping and the CPC: the CPC must ensure a fair and equitable society where upward social and economic mobility remains part of the social contract between the Chinese people and the government. It is unfair that one or two families in a village can get unimaginably wealthy for generations while others cannot even access the land or capital needed to create companies in the first place, let alone generate wealth.

If China does not address this growing wealth inequality, mainland Chinese will eventually feel the same levels of frustration and anger felt by many in Hong Kong, which many believe led to the Hong Kong Riots of 2019 more than a real push for democracy.

Xi's Common Prosperity is not a return to a 1960s-style economy—no Cultural Revolution 2.0 marked by violence and social upheaval. Common Prosperity is about ensuring poor people in China can become middle class. Common Prosperity is also about preventing the growth of multi-generational wealth like in Hong Kong where Li Ka-shing and similar tycoons lord it over the city.

It was unfair that only people like Pierre and Isabelle, the offspring of the 10 percent, could obtain access to the best tutors and schools. Today, the aim is rather to increase opportunity and remove obstacles to improving one's chances in life for all, not just the select few.

For the most part, the families of people like Pierre and Isabelle have gotten wealthy not by doing anything wrong or illegal. There was perhaps some corruption 20 years ago as officials forced them to be corrupt, but families have become professional in their operations as the government cracks down on corruption. Broader questions remain: How does the government maintain the rule of law and curb excess power and domination by a small group of citizens? What regulations are needed to ensure confidence in capital expenditure remains intact? How does the government hold these officials and businesspeople accountable for corrupt actions decades ago without destroying the "animal spirits" needed in the present to drive the economy.

By cracking down on the tech and education sectors, the government hopes to make society fairer and more equitable. The downside is that among the 10 percent across China—from Tier 1 cities all the way to smaller cities—there is increasing pressure to emigrate and move capital out of the country. Pierre confided in me that he has illegally received a Canadian passport while retaining his Chinese one. He did this, he said, "just in case." Princess applied for a Singaporean passport for her whole family just in case things went south.

Rising uncertainty and disquiet among the 10 percent in the face of the country's sharp turn toward socialism is causing them to sell properties at a discount and to transfer capital offshore—often illegally through cryptocurrencies like Bitcoin or money launderers based in Hong Kong and Macau. Panic selling is causing real estate prices to soften.

As the government tries to ensure equal opportunities across the board in China, it needs to ensure that it does not hamper risk takers' ability to make money or make them lose their animal spirits. If the government is too heavy-handed in its laudable move for a fairer society, top business minds will simply retire, wait until the political winds are more favorable again before investing again, or move their companies to other countries.

One immigration lawyer in Shanghai told me, "I am crazy busy helping the rich secure new citizenships. They are all trying to immigrate to other countries like the US or Canada. They worry the Chinese government will crack down and take away all their wealth."

How to deal with the *fuerdai* is another emerging issue. The first generation of entrepreneurs who gained significant wealth were often hardworking but their children, on the other hand, are not often focused on business endeavors. There are no inheritance taxes. A starting salary for an Ivy League-educated person in Beijing is between 1000–3000 USD per month, so why would people like Pierre work hard to make 2000 USD a month when their family is worth billions? Isabelle told me that her husband just sits around the house and factory and plays with friends because there is nothing really for him to do. His father and employees did all the hard work while her husband just played and spent money. With all their money and free time, Pierre and Isabelle's husband offer great opportunities for luxury brands and private wealth management firms to cater to their needs, as well as real estate players outside of China.

For luxury brands, these young *fuerdai* present huge opportunities. They often want the best and will pay to have goods customized to meet their whims. They are sophisticated shoppers who are well traveled and have studied internationally. Brands need to learn what motivates these *fuerdai* to make purchases and how to create emotional connections.

Many *fuerdai* feel their parents do not take them seriously as businesspeople. Older generations still control the decision-making when it comes to business. As one executive working for a billionaire told me, "The big boss's son works in the company. He is in his early thirties, and clearly the father does not respect his business acumen. So none of us listen to the 'little boss.' It is sad as he just sits around doing nothing except spending money. The tension between the father and son is palpable."

Note

1. "Per Capita Gross Domestic Product (GDP) in China 2022, by Region," *Statista*, March 1, 2023, https://www.statista.com/statistics/1093666/china-per-capita-gross-domestic-product-gdp-by-province/

CHAPTER 13

The Hong Kong Riots, Taiwan, and Greater Bay Area Integration

"I challenge you to condemn the bigoted violence on mainland Chinese." With these words I confronted Joshua Wong during a debate between him and me organized by *The Economist* in Hong Kong in October 2019.[1] Medium height with a squarish build, Joshua is the most famous prodemocracy Hong Kong activist since the territory returned to mainland Chinese control in 1997. Until that year, Hong Kong had been a British colony, ceded by Qing-dynasty China to the British Empire under the terms of the Treaty of Nanjing, at the close of the First Opium War in 1842.

Joshua rose to fame as a teenager when he became the face of the largely peaceful Umbrella Protests in 2014. The world media flocked to hear his calls for democracy and religious freedom and his criticism of communist rule. During the 2019 riots in Hong Kong, he took on an equally high-profile role in the Western media but was not the leader of the protests—indeed, no one took credit for leading the protests. Famous protesters like Joshua, Denise Ho, Joey Siu, Nathan Law, and Jimmy Lai all claim that the protests grew organically, and that no one was at the head.

The day before my debate with Joshua, the violence in Hong Kong had escalated, including the throwing of Molotov cocktails, so *The Economist* scaled down the event. Originally, it had expected a thousand attendees but, because of fears over violence, had reduced the number of attendees to several dozen, including the speakers, *Economist* staff, and a few select others. There had been an attack on a mainland Chinese who worked for J.P. Morgan. The banker had been assaulted after shouting "We are all Chinese!", referring to Hong Kongers and mainlanders. The attack on the banker showed the ethnic animosity coursing through the protests. Protesters looked down upon mainlanders as uncouth and uncivilized and did not want people to suggest that Hong Kongers came from the same ethnic stock.

Portrayed as righteous by the US media, it might surprise some that Joshua refused to condemn the bigoted attacks on mainland Chinese. After all, isn't Joshua supposed to be a human rights activist?

Joshua's response disappointed me as I had hoped Joshua was a true fighter for human rights:

"We know the tension between the protestors and Mainlanders happens in the past few months yes, is not the first incident and not the first accident that no one hopes will happen. I will say that instead of condemn any behavior of protestors, I prefer to find another solution through another process to let us realize that even protestor have self-protection. How to use force and maintain public support is a matter for us."[2]

Joshua refused to condemn bigoted violence on mainland Chinese. Think about the backlash against Brooklyn Nets star Kyrie Irving for tweeting a link to the 2018 movie *Hebrews to Negroes: Wake Up Black America* that many in the Jewish community viewed as antisemitic. He was suspended without pay for five games and had to meet with the Anti-Defamation League and Jewish community leaders before he could be reinstated.

US media touted Joshua as righteous,[3] even though he would not criticize violence against people who had done nothing wrong but be born on the mainland. He has been nominated for the Nobel Peace Prize, and the US Speaker of the House of Representatives, Nancy Pelosi (a Democrat from California), as well as Senators Tom Cotton (a Republican from Arkansas), Marco Rubio (a Republican from Florida), and Joshua Hawley (a Republican from Missouri), rushed to meet him and express solidarity with his cause. *Fortune* named him as one of the world's "50 Greatest Leaders" in 2015.[4]

Through omission, the US media did not accurately portray the violence of the riots that Joshua had failed to condemn. Hong Kong's airport was occupied by rioters, and they took a *Global Times* journalist, Fu Guohao, hostage because he was from the mainland. Fu later suffered from depression and eventually died by suicide, in part because of his ordeal.

Terrorists lobbed Molotov cocktails at Hong Kong police and destroyed subway tracks. Gangs of male youth prowled around the city with long, metal pipes and attacked police and people suspected of supporting Beijing. They firebombed and destroyed establishments like Starbucks because the daughter of the founder of Starbuck's Hong Kong licensee had spoken out in support of Beijing.

Not all of the protesters were violent to be sure, but a large number were, which was not adequately presented in US media coverage. I interviewed dozens of peaceful protesters and violent rioters—I found bigotry and economic frustration fueled much of the protests more than a demand for democracy.

Few Western media accounts covered the underlying bigotry coursing through the movement or the role that intolerant evangelical Christianity played. Many rioters were extreme Christians who look down upon nonbelievers: they liken mainlanders to locusts for their lack of religious beliefs. Like Australian prime minister Scott Morrison, human rights activist Adrian Zenz, who is behind many of the allegations about forced labor and genocide in Xinjiang, and American secretary of state Mike Pompeo, Joshua Wong practices a form of intolerant Christianity that does not allow for a clear separation of Church and State.

The protesters I interviewed were also pessimistic about their economic futures and this fueled a lot of anger. House prices and rents were too high, good jobs sparse, and wealth concentrated within a small British and Hong Kong elite.

Grievances such as unaffordable housing were legitimate, as was the desire to ensure the Hong Kong way of life, language, and culture, along with freedom of speech and freedom of the press. Protesters worried the press would become a tool of the government, as on the mainland. Resolving these legitimate issues and concerns is key to ensuring Hong Kong could remain one of the world's great cities and leading financial centers.

Fighting for democracy

I made my way through the swelling crowd of protesters to the very front to where rioters clad all in black were throwing Molotov cocktails at police in front of their Admiralty headquarters. I asked one of the rioters how old he was. He said he was 18.

I asked, "What are your goals?" and he responded, his voice muffled by the gas mask he wore, "We're fighting for our freedom. We're fighting for democracy!" He pumped his fists. He sounded as though he was reciting soundbites for television cameras.

What freedom was he lacking? I thought to myself. Hong Kong, after all, had ranked number 30 on the Human Freedom Index in 2021, while the US and UK were tied at 15.[5] Hong Kong had long enjoyed its position as one of the most vibrant and free societies in the world, with individual income tax capped at 17 percent. Twitter, Facebook, and even Telegram were accessible in Hong Kong—mainland authorities had left the internet free in Hong Kong unlike on the mainland where VPNs are needed to access many non-mainland Chinese websites.

Some of Hong Kong's freedoms have arguably disappeared in the years since the 2020 implementation of the "national security law" (NSL), the Law of the People's Republic of China on Safeguarding National Security in the Hong Kong Special Administrative Region (HKSAR). However, it is clear the Chinese government is content to keep the One Country Two Systems policy in place but had to act and implement the NSL, which has similarities to bills and laws in the UK and US, in order to stop violence.

Hong Kong still largely has freedom of the press and an uncensored internet but has cracked down on activists, like Joshua and Jimmy Lai, collaborating with foreign powers to try to overthrow the political system.

What country in the world would allow its legislature to be stormed or its airport to be shut down by rioters? What country in the world would allow protesters to throw Molotov cocktails at the police and subway tracks for months on end? What country would allow a movement intended to overthrow the political system? Sunak would not in the UK, neither would Biden in the US. Something had to be done in Hong Kong to stop the violence. The US has jailed dozens of rioters who stormed Capitol Hill, some for over ten years, with some lawmakers arguing Donald Trump himself should be investigated and punished for encouraging the violence.

After interviewing a terrorist who had thrown Molotov cocktails, I interviewed one tall, lanky 25-year-old and his friends who were among the peaceful protesters. He represented the majority of protesters who were angry but did not engage in violence. I asked, "Do you think it's right for the rioters to incite violence on just mainland Chinese individuals and mainland Chinese-owned business?"

He scowled. "We hate mainlanders. They're not like us. We are embarrassed when people says that Hong Kongers and mainlanders are both Chinese. We are not like them at all. They are inferior to us. They defecate on the street. They are below us." His friends nodded up and down in agreement. None of them even mentioned the word "democracy" during our 20-minute interview.

Many of the violent protesters fought with the vague notion of freedom or democracy in their heads. All of the violent protesters I interviewed mentioned the term "democracy." None was able to articulate what that meant exactly, but the fight for democracy seemed to be a rallying call for people to join the protests. They also used the phrase "the fight for democracy and freedom" as if the slogans were rehearsed for Western media cameras.

In my interviews, I did find bigotry against mainlanders coursing through the protests. In interview after interview,

Hong Kongers clearly resented being under the political control of people they considered poor and uncivilized.

Solving problems through economic support

How to integrate Hong Kong into the mainland without seeing a return of rioting and how to reunify Taiwan with China peacefully are two key challenges facing China. However, they also provide opportunities for businesses that understand government plans to reduce the anger by giving Hong Kong's lower and middle classes more economic opportunities for integrating Hong Kong's economy into the area of southern China known as the Greater Bay Area (GBA).

In Tibet and Xinjiang, China has been fairly successful in winning over minority populations like Uyghurs, Tibetans, and Kazakhs by expanding access to health care and education and improving the economy through infrastructure spending. Throwing money at problems has worked well in these regions, as we saw with the Uyghur family that had just seen the birth of their daughter or with the 42-year old Tibetan Party secretary, because the people were so poor that getting them food and shelter bred support and loyalty. Businesses, often non-Han Chinese–owned, that invest in regions like Tibet and Xinjiang in sectors like infrastructure and travel and leisure have profited from helping to jump-start economies there. These regions have also seen decades of shared history, education, and government under the CPC since 1949 so different ethnic groups have coexisted in one nation for generations now.

The challenges facing Beijing when it comes to Hong Kong and Taiwan are not as easily resolved—both were colonized by other powers during the lifetime of many citizens—the UK and Japan, respectively. The populations have been influenced by different cultures, education systems, religions, and political systems. Hong Kong only reverted back to mainland control in 1997 so a large percentage of the population grew up during British colonial rule. Taiwan has been supported both economically and militarily by America since 1949, after the effective end of Japanese colonial rule in 1945. The Chinese Civil War caused Taiwan and the mainland to be enemies, often distrustful of each other.

Elites in Hong Kong and Taiwan have close ties with their former colonizers and Western nations through long-standing business and education relations. The middle class in Hong Kong and Taiwan often send children to their former colonizers to pursue their educations.

The role religion plays in causing a cleavage between the mainland and Hong Kong and Taiwan should not be underestimated. Cardinal Joseph Zen from Hong Kong has long condemned the CPC and has even criticized the pope and the Vatican City for forging stronger relations with Beijing. Many in Zen's flock believe it is their religious duty to oppose the Communist Party.

Taiwanese and Hong Kongers are wealthier than mainlanders, so throwing money at these territories won't fix as many problems. In Hong Kong, the average per capita GDP in 2019 was four times higher than on the mainland, where it is 48,356 USD, versus mainland China's 10,144 USD.[6] Throwing money around is not necessarily going to be a similar panacea as it was for poorer regions of the mainland like Tibet and Xinjiang.

One question businesspeople often ask me is whether a war will break out over Taiwan. Many worry Xi will resort to force to reunify Taiwan and China. Worries over armed conflict have caused businesses to defer investing in case a war over Taiwan breaks out and they are forced to shut, as happened in Russia after it invaded Ukraine—Pizza Hut, Hyatt, and Marriott all shut down their entire Russian operations due to public and government pressure in the US.

Many Chinese feel the US is trying to provoke a proxy war over Taiwan. They point to visits to Taiwan in recent years by American politicians like Nancy Pelosi, Mike Pompeo, and Mike Gallagher. Biden has said on three different occasions that the US would support Taiwan militarily, only for White House spokespeople to backtrack on his statements.

President Tsai in Taiwan increased the mandatory enlistment period for Taiwanese males from four months to one year in December 2022. Beijing views extended mandatory enlistment and weapon purchases from American weapon manufacturers like Lockheed Martin as provocations by the Taiwanese. America also announced it would permanently base special forces on Taiwan's Kinmen Island, just a few kilometers from the mainland. That would be equivalent to China basing soldiers on Key Largo. To Taiwanese and DC, the moves are defensive measures meant to deter the mainland from invading.

Businesspeople need to be aware of the nuances of the historical background between the mainland and Hong Kong and Taiwan or else they might run afoul of mainland authorities and consumers or be criticized by American and Taiwanese politicians for kowtowing to Chinese government demands. CEOs of even SMEs have to become well-schooled in the historical relationships, to smooth over differences, and act as a senior diplomat of sorts so as to placate all sides. If companies do not understand the political sensitivities, they can lose serious money and market share by making geopolitical missteps.

Through initiatives like the Greater Bay and Hong Kong economic integration, as well as tax incentives and other subsidies for Taiwanese investing in Fujian Province, Beijing plans to use the same playbook that worked in Tibet and Xinjiang to gain popular support from Hong Kongers and Taiwanese—they will invest in infrastructure and housing in these regions and give education and health care benefits to help alleviate poverty.

An unequal society

No fair observer of Hong Kong could call its society fair or that equal opportunities exist for citizens. Ten families control a huge portion of the economy: rumor has it almost 7 percent of every dollar spent goes to the Li Ka-sheng's business entities alone. Wealth concentration has prevented upward economic mobility. The concentration of wealth limits the futures of young people. Hundreds of thousands have immigrated in recent years to the UK, Canada, and Australia in search of better economic opportunities, and out of anger at both the Hong Kong and Beijing governments.

British colonialism drove the wealth cleavage by giving opportunities to British entities and a few favored local families during colonization. Conglomerates owned by British like Swire Pacific and Jardine Matheson emerged during colonial rule and maintain economic dominance to this day, in everything from beverages to autos to real estate. A few locals collaborated with the British grew wealthy by helping them maintain control over the local population.

When Hong Kong reverted back to Chinese control, Hong Kong businesspeople fled to Canada as they worried the communists would destroy their businesses. Many of my class-mates at McGill were Hong Kongers who had immigrated to Vancouver out of fear of the communists. However, instead of destroying the economy, Beijing pushed hard to show the world Hong Kong was still open for business. Instead of appointing a governor or mayor of Hong Kong, they called the top position in the territory the "chief executive."

Beijing gave the Hong Kong tycoons opportunities in mainland China to develop tracts of prime real estate at cheap rates. Tycoon-owned companies like the Hong Kong New World Group, Sun Hung Kai Properties, and Li Ka-shing's Hutchison Whampoa, scooped up key real estate throughout the country on the cheap with the support of Beijing.

Rather than being hurt by communist rule, Hong Kong tycoons benefited from the mainland Chinese real estate boom. Li Ka-shing built Oriental Plaza in the heart of Beijing on Wangfujing Dajie, the Cheng family that controls the New World Group owns the K11 Hong Kong towers on Shanghai's Huaihai Road, Vincent Lo's Shui On Group built Shanghai's Xintiandi, Ronnie and Gerald Chan of Hang Lung Group built Plaza 66 on Shanghai's Nanjing Road and the Grand Gateway in the Xujiahui part of Shanghai. During the Jiang Zemin era, the government felt that, if it continued to help Li Ka-shing be "superman," this would placate the everyday Hong Kongers who idolized the tycoons.

Gaining the support of the tycoons worked well at first for Beijing. China showed it was open for business, and global investment flooded into China, with Hong Kong as the conduit. But Beijing did not put in measures to ensure the prosperity in Hong Kong was enjoyed by the lower and middle classes. A widening economic gap emerged between the wealthy and everyday Hong Kongers, causing frustration and anger. Poor Hong Kongers live in cage-like nano-sized flats at 163 square feet. High real estate costs prevented Hong Kongers from becoming entrepreneurs. They simply took jobs at tycoon-owned companies to pay the bills.

Hong Kong's government raised most revenue through land sales and maintained a low-income tax rate to support the finance sector. The amount of land open for development was kept in the hands of real estate tycoons who did not want to develop too much to maintain the value of their landbanks. Little affordable housing was built.

By the time the mass protests hit Hong Kong in 2019, it was clear to Beijing that the best way to resolve problems was to focus on improving the economy for lower- and middle-income Hong Kongers and curtail the power of tycoons like Li Kai-shing.

Lessons from the riots

The lessons Beijing authorities took from the Hong Kong riots was that they had to support the growth of the middle class and stop wealth and power from being concentrated in the hands of the tycoons. In other words, Hong Kong would benefit from a Common Prosperity-like drive. Reading the tea leaves, Li Kai-shing divested his mainland holdings. He sold almost everything on the mainland and reallocated investments to Europe. The era of tycoon dominance in the Chinese economy came to an end under Xi.

Beijing is following the well-worn playbook of throwing money at a problem when they see one, a playbook that has worked well on the mainland. To support a more equitable society, China announced plans to build more affordable housing in the New Territories part of Hong Kong. They also pushed China's initiative to integrate Hong Kong into the Greater Bay Area (GBA) in Guangdong Province. Policies give incentives to Hong Kongers who invest in the region through tax breaks and other initiatives. Hong Kongers can buy homes and retire in the GBA even when cities do not allow mainlanders from other cities to buy homes there. The mainland government also gives Hong Kongers preferential treatment for school and university places in mainland China.

Hong Kong will benefit economically by being the conduit to the GBA. Smart money is going to the GBA. The daughter of a billionaire Hong Kong tycoon told me she planned to invest 300 million USD solely in the GBA including Hong Kong because the opportunities to integrate the economies of the Pearl River Delta with Hong Kong are enormous.

Taiwan

While the mainland can support integration between Hong Kong and southern China easily because it formally controls both, Taiwan will be harder to solve in the short term as Beijing does not have direct control over Taipei. But China is trying to rely on the same playbook to gain popular support among Taiwanese in the hope for a peaceful unification.

Beijing announced it would streamline Taiwanese investment into Fujian Province and make it easier for Taiwanese to buy homes and go to school there. They streamlined the application process for Taiwanese to apply to universities in Fujian. These incentives and policies show Xi does not want to use force to unify Taiwan and the mainland anytime soon. Many fearmongers like political scientist Hal Brands argue

China might attack Taiwan to divert attention away from the weak economy in the post-Covid era. That does not make sense. The end of 2022 would have been a good time to divert attention from the rising tide of anger at draconian zero-Covid policies and a weak economy, but Xi made no moves toward using the military against Taiwan.

It is clear Xi wants to formally take control of Taiwan and won't rule out using military force—no president will ever rule that out—but it is also clear Xi does not plan to use force anytime soon. He has used strident words but that is nothing new—his words mirror those Chinese leaders have used for 75 years since Chiang Kai-Shek and the Nationalists fled to Taiwan. Instead, Xi wants to rely on the playbook he used in Tibet and Xinjiang to gain popular support from Hong Kongers and Taiwanese and reach his objectives that way—peacefully.

In the near term, the risk of a war in Taiwan centers around an unplanned incident such as when a US spy plane crashed into a Chinese fighter jet off the coast of Hainan Island in 2001 or around a provocation by America to lure China into a proxy war. But former Chinese ambassador to America Cui Tiankai has said that China isn't stupid and would not be duped into a proxy war with America over Taiwan.

Businesses will benefit from the mainland's policies supporting Hong Kong's and Taiwan's integration into the mainland economy to reduce tension. Businesses that help support poverty alleviation in Hong Kong, similar to China's Common Prosperity Drive, will benefit the most as China seeks to increase the size of the middle class in Hong Kong and Taiwan through investments in health care, education, and affordable housing.

Notes

1. *The Economist*, Shaun Rein Debates Joshua Wong, Open Future Forum in Hong Kong, October 5, 2019, available at https://www.youtube.com/watch?v=UlKSM_yumaw
2. Ibid.
3. Mark Jenkins, "Youthful Protest Gets Serious in Joshua: Teenager vs. Superpower," *NPR*, May 26, 2017. https://www.npr.org/2017/05/26/529672042/youthful-protest-gets-serious-in-joshua-teenager-vs-superpower
4. Fortune. "The Worlds 50 Greatest Leaders" *Fortune*. April 2015.
5. Ian Vasquez, Fred McMahon, Ryan Murphy, and Guillermina Sutter Schneider, "The Human Freedom Index 2021," *The Frasier Institute*, 2021, https://www.fraserinstitute.org/sites/default/files/human-freedom-index-2021.pdf
6. "GDP Hong Kong SAR, China," *World Bank Data*, https://data.worldbank.org/indicator/NY.GDP.MKTP.CD?locations=HK

CHAPTER 14

Chinese Youth

Lying Flat (Tanping)

"My sister refuses to look for work," Jasmine, a 27-year-old accountant in Beijing told me. Jasmine was worried that her younger sister had lost her way in life. She did not have any career goals—most of the time she stayed in her room at her parents' apartment watching online video clips or going out with friends to coffee shops. Every few months she toured around China with friends—paid for by her parents.

This was not the life her parents envisioned for her when they sent Jasmine and her sister to study in America. Their father was a senior executive in China for a Fortune 500 firm, and they had big plans for both daughters. When Jasmine returned to China, she took a job after graduation with a prestigious accounting firm and moved to her own apartment. Her sister moved back in with her parents and sat around the house. "My sister refuses to look for work. My mother pays her a monthly allowance to take care of my parents and run errands!"

The lingering impact on mental health from zero-Covid restrictions, a PTSD of sorts, combined with fears over geopolitical tension, has eroded the work ethic of many Chinese youth and created a wholesale change in their behavior. Unlike the optimistic youth who drove sales of luxury goods and restaurant meals before Covid, young Chinese today are anxious and stressed and have started to reprioritize what they think is important in life. Instead of working hard like young people did during the go-go days so they could buy Louis Vuitton handbags and Porsche cars, youth are now lying flat (*tanping*) and trading down on purchases. They do not see how they can get wealthy so they do not work hard or prioritize their careers. Anxious over their futures, young people are looking for discounts and have little brand loyalty. They don't care if brands are foreign or domestic—just whether they are good value. When they do trade up, it is for limited categories such as saving up to spend on experiences like traveling, sports activities like boxing, Pilates and yoga, and on product categories they deem valuable such as outdoor and sports apparel.

My friend hired a young man, David, who studied in the US for high school and college. He took a year off after graduation to hang out with friends and travel around China. I asked him why he had not looked for work for a full year, and he told me that because of Covid he had not been back to China for three years so wanted to spend time catching up with his parents and friends. Besides, the job market was bad, so he decided to wait until the next recruiting season in hopes of finding a better job.

Won over by his intelligence, despite concerns over the gap in his résumé, my friend offered David a job. Everything went downhill quickly. David asked to defer his start for three months because he wanted to take his girlfriend to Dubai. When David finally did join, he was smart but quit after one week because he did not want to work late or travel on business. David told my friend he wanted to spend more time with his girlfriend, so no longer wanted to work.

David quit at a time when young people are supposedly facing an unemployment problem. Unlike what you read in US media, the reality is that there are jobs, but young people refuse to take them because they do not want to work hard, or they want to wait for the perfect job and salary.

For Chinese born after 1998, the ideal life differs from that of those born just a few years earlier. Many have parents who can afford to cover or supplement the cost of their children's lives, as with Jasmine's sister. Starting salaries are low, even for graduates of prestigious schools in America and China. Because many parents did not spend much time with their children during Covid, they are willing to give them an allowance, whether they are employed or not, to make their lives more comfortable. As one young woman with a full-time job told me, "My parents give me several hundred USD a month to supplement my salary." A father of a 22-year-old white-collar worker told me, "Only bad parents don't pay for their children's rent since salaries are so low."

Aside from not prioritizing their careers, many young people do not want marry early, or even at all. The number of marriages registered in 2022 dropped 50 percent year over year and the number of babies born plummeted to 9 million, down from 16 million in 2015.[1] The low rates are partially due to Covid but are part of a long-term trend of Chinese marrying later. *The Global Times* reports that in 2022 people aged 25–29 made up the largest ratio getting married 37.24 percent while the ratio of 20–24-year-olds registering marriage dropped to 15.2 percent in 2022, down from 37.6 percent in 2010.[2]

Since the end of the Covid era, thoughts about work and marriage have shifted. Chinese youth have changed priorities and outlook at life. One young woman I interviewed from Henan told me her mother said she should wait until her thirties to get married, if she even wanted to get married at all. Brands need to understand these emerging trends and change their marketing strategies. Marketing campaigns targeting young people should no longer be about aspiring to be rich but about wanting to live unique, often niche, lifestyles with an emphasis on well-being. Some youth buy streetwear to appear edgy; others get their footwear from Hoka to look cool and athletic; others dye their hair to look punk. This shift provides opportunities for smaller, niche brands to expand into China and carve out strong market positions. No one brand will dominate market share anymore, like in the early 2000s when brands like Zegna and Omega controlled 70 percent of their sectors. No longer wanting to be like everyone else, Chinese spend money to express their own unique values and preferences.

What caused China's young people to start to lie flat and not focus on their careers and making money as much as previous generations? What caused them to want to marry later or not marry at all? The lying flat trend stems partly from the weak economy and geopolitical tension outlined in this book so far, but a greater part derives from their experience during the implementation of zero-Covid policies at the local level. Policies limited personal freedom and caused hopelessness and anxiety, so young people prioritized mental and physical well-being.

Everything marketers and investors thought they knew about Chinese youth in the pre-Covid days has to be thrown out because of the monumental shift in consumer habits— young people are no longer the optimistic force like they were in the pre-Covid days when they bought on credit to trade up and buy what everyone else coveted. China's young people now have more anxiety than at any time since the 1978 economic reforms.

Frustration over zero-Covid

By the end of October 2022, after suffering almost three years of limitations on their mobility due to zero-Covid policies that were meant to keep them safe and healthy, consumer confidence among Chinese youth collapsed. Anxious over their futures, they began to trade down in their purchases, ending a decade of premiumization in buying habits by previous generations of youth. Frustrated at the implementation of zero-Covid at the local level, some young people made the almost unheard-of decision to protest publicly against zero-Covid policies. In all my decades in China, I had not seen such widespread protests against government policies before.

The sometimes haphazard implementation of zero-Covid at the local level hurt young people's confidence. Instead of purchasing luxury products or drinking expensive coffees with friends at Starbucks to display a lifestyle of success and underscore their confidence that they would one day be rich, zero-Covid made Chinese youth rethink their spending patterns. They began to look for discounts rather than buy out of brand loyalty. Instead of being loyal to a coffee brand like Costa or Starbucks, they would buy whatever coffee was cheapest that day, switching coffee shops daily depending upon promotions. If they did buy luxury products, it was not out of confidence that they would eventually make it big, but as a nondrug way to feel better and relieve stress for a few hours.

Meant to ensure the safety of its citizens, Xi's dynamic zero-Covid policies in 2020 and 2021 were run brilliantly and saved lives—while the rest of the world quarantined, Chinese could still eat out in restaurants in large groups, mask wearing was generally optional, and domestic travel was easy, even if international borders were shut. But policies starting in March 2022 during the Shanghai lockdown and then countrywide policies in August 2022 that required regular Covid testing wreaked havoc on business and on the mental health of China's citizens. Policies often no longer made sense, or were implemented draconianly and hurt youth consumer confidence.

Poor local implementation

Local officialdom's fear of letting Covid spread rose to a fever pitch after the Shanghai lockdown. Officials never got reprimanded by Beijing if they were heavy-handed in trying to contain Covid but they were for being too relaxed. Out of self-preservation, local officials typically erred on the side of being draconian on policies. Schools in some cities switched to online learning even if there was not a single Covid case in the entire city, causing scheduling problems for working parents and hurting the education and socialization of children. My son went six months without seeing a classmate in person. Even after Shanghai's liberation, my son's school would do in-person learning for one to two weeks then online for a week, and back and forth for over a semester, at the whim of local education officials worried about the spread of Covid.

The population was forced to take regular PCR Covid tests, sometimes every 24 hours, to be allowed into malls, restaurants, and hospitals. Getting a Covid test often meant queuing for hours at a time in rain and blizzards. Guards in housing compounds forced residents to show green health codes to be allowed into their own homes.

University students got hit especially hard by Covid policies because of fears Covid would spread through tightly packed dorms where often four to six students lived in one room. Universities forbade students from leaving campuses to dine out or even search for jobs. Many universities stopped students from leaving campus during the entire school year for any reason whatsoever. Many students felt like prisoners on their college campuses. After the Shanghai lockdown, local officials often no longer seemed scientific in their implementation of zero-Covid as they had in 2020 and 2021.

Young people worried about getting sick from even regular illnesses because they would not be allowed to see a doctor unless they had had a Covid test. During the Shanghai lockdown, people died from heart attacks and other illnesses because hospitals refused to admit them until they had recent Covid test results. Pregnant women had problems getting the paperwork approved necessary to see doctors. My son almost lost his eyesight after he got hit in the eye—the hospital wouldn't treat him because we didn't take along his mobile phone with his health code on it when we rushed to the hospital at 1 a.m. We had to use my phone to log in to his account, delaying access to treatment—the doctor said a longer delay might have left my son blind. With all the rules on testing to be allowed into hospitals, schools, airplanes, and even into one's own home, life had become Kafkaesque, causing mental health problems. One white paper from a government affiliated think tank found nearly 50 percent of Shanghainese suffered from anxiety and/or depression due to the Shanghai lockdown.[3]

The central government after the 20th People's Congress in October 2022 ordered local governments not to be too strict in applying policies—Beijing ordered governments to stop tracing and locking down close contacts of close contacts. Until then, young people were scared to go out to a mall because thousands of people who visited a mall could be quarantined if just one person with Covid entered the mall.

Beijing also ordered local governments to become more scientific in how they decided what parts of the city to lock down, and to lock down individual floors or buildings rather than entire compounds and districts if one Covid case was found.

Worried about letting Covid spread and getting into trouble, many local governments kept harsh policies in place, however. Shanghai actually increased testing requirements from 72 hours to 48 hours for office buildings and restaurants. Visitors from other cities were not allowed to go into a mall or a restaurant for five days but, in an obviously unscientific policy that further frustrated young people, were still allowed to take public transportation and go into office buildings.

The constant testing and use of health codes, combined with the difficulty in searching for jobs, took a toll on the mental health of young people. My firm tried to hire recent college graduates, but often interviewees canceled last minute if they were coming from other cities because travel policies were too onerous and fast-changing. Traveling within China at that time was stressful, so I didn't blame them. On one business trip, I had green health codes from both Qingdao and Shanghai but neither were accepted when I visited Wuhan. I had three PCR test results from the previous 72 hours from Qingdao and a test from Wuhan itself at the airport but was stopped at a roadside checkpoint in Wuhan.

The person in charge of the checkpoint wanted a Wuhan green code before I could pass. But in Wuhan, foreigners needed to arrive at their hotel and get permission from local police before a green code was issued. The local public security bureau (PSB) told me to expect to wait 72 hours before I got approval. Until then, I could only get a grey code. The boss of the checkpoint would not let me pass. He said, "I determine the rules for this checkpoint and you cannot pass. I got stuck on that highway for hours, not allowed to go back to the airport or forward to my hotel, until the check-point boss finally relented and let me pass.

Each province, city, district, and, in some cases, individual street checkpoints had different rules on how to pass. The economy dropped to a standstill. Young people could not interview for jobs or go out with friends to restaurants stress-free. They often just stayed in the rooms and communicated with friends via apps. Young people felt as though they had no control over their lives and, unable to find jobs, no hope for the future.

Local officials like the head of that checkpoint had total power over our daily lives. Neighborhood committees could determine who was locked down, who could enter housing compounds, and whether couriers were allowed to deliver food. Committees made decisions out of fear of making a mistake and making those higher up angry. For them, it was better to be harsh rather than let Covid spread.

Adding to the frustration were livestreams by fans at the World Cup in Qatar in November 2022 that showed tens of thousands of maskless, sweaty fans crowding the stadium. State-owned media downplayed the scenes, but the Chinese youth who saw the crowds on livestreams wondered whether Covid really was still serious. Youth-led protests erupted across the country driven by young people fed up with the restrictions.

Within weeks of the protests, Covid spread around the country. Unable to stop the spread, seemingly overnight the central government rescinded all Covid restrictions. The speed of the opening up was so fast and so unexpected that it caused a great deal of fear among young people and throughout the population because they had been conditioned to think Covid would cause death even to the young and healthy. There were shortages of fever-reducing medicines like ibuprofen and paracetamol as well as Covid-specific medicines like Paxlovid. ICU beds in hospitals, too, were in short supply.

Cities became ghost towns as consumers were too scared to venture out of their homes even though there was happiness that zero-Covid had ended. Young people did not go out and revenge-spend and party like their peers did in America when Covid policies were lifted—they were too tired, too anxious, and too worried about money to go out and spend. They kept saving for rainy days.

No revenge spending

After zero-Covid ended, J.P. Morgan and Goldman Sachs predicted young people would revenge-spend in China. But Wall Street underestimated how anxious young people were over their economic futures, which is why there was no revenge spending. During Covid, companies had often cut salaries or furloughed workers without pay for months on end. One general manager of a major hotel chain told me that "40 percent of my junior workers have been on unpaid furlough for months. My employees are stressed out over the lack of pay, but there is nothing I can do."

Once optimistic, and sure that they would make a lot of money and lead better lives than their parents, youth are now pessimistic after facing years of low salaries. Bonuses in the post-Covid era have also not rebounded to 2019 levels. Even with housing prices throughout the country softening, prices are still far too high for most young people to even consider getting a house unless their parents help pay for it. More and more young people tell me they feel there is "no hope" for the future.

Dealing with so much stress and fears of their economic futures, Chinese youth are reassessing what they value in life and how to allocate spending budgets: they have shifted from wanting to show off by buying luxury items to focusing on stress reduction to improve mental health and wellness. They are turning toward religion and spirituality to find meaning in life. The number of young people practicing Christianity, Daoism, and Buddhism is all rising. Many have taken up meditation.

Before Covid, Chinese youth bought items to show off. They wanted to buy luxury products to show the world that they were sophisticated and worldly and on the way up the social ladder. Buying a luxury handbag meant they had made it. As one 28-year-old from Jiangsu told me in 2012 that she had skipped lunch for six months so she could afford a Giorgio Armani coat. She told me she would take a bus rather than a taxi to save enough money to buy luxury items. Spending for her and many of her generation at the time was all about showing that one could afford luxury and that they had scraped their way out of abject poverty.

In the post-Covid era, young people are skipping buying luxury items and trading down, buying cheaper cosmetics from local brands like Proya, and unbranded bags and clothes straight from factories via online sites like Pinduoduo and Douyin that are as much as 95 percent cheaper than their luxury equivalents but which still look good and stylish enough. Why spend thousands of renminbi for shoes from Manolo Blahnik when you can buy a stylish one for 100 RMB direct from a factory?

As product quality has improved, there is no longer the need to buy brand names to look good and stylish anymore. Brands with mid-tier positioning like Gap or H&M have become irrelevant. Youth now purchase products as part of curating a lifestyle where they display their own sense of creativity, individuality, and uniqueness. Spending is becoming more and more for consumers' own "self-happiness," about defining who they are. Typically, it is more the *fuerdai* like Pierre and Princess who buy luxury items—you do not see young people in the 90 percent skipping lunch for six months like that young woman from Jiangsu to buy a luxury handbag anymore.

Exercise- and beauty-related products are categories Chinese youth are most willing to spend on. Women especially are spending more on yoga, Pilates, and even boxing. There is increased spending on yoga clothes and sports apparel from Lululemon, On, and Hoka at the high end, to more general workout clothes from domestic Chinese brands like Xtep. Chinese want to look and feel good while exercising.

Spending more on oneself for self-happiness by Chinese youth will continue for the foreseeable future. Much like the Great Depression changed the spending habits for a lifetime of Americans who were children during it (my grandmother who was born in 1917 reused aluminum foil to the day she died in her eighties), habits will forever be altered for young people who suffered through zero-Covid policies, Rather than showing off they can afford a luxury handbag, they are showing off that they are fit and healthy by posting photos and videos of themselves exercising on WeChat Moments and Douyin.

The rise of fitness classes

After the stress of Covid and to help relieve my back pain (I had back surgery when I was a teenager and was in a body cast for a year and used a cane for five years), I decided to try my first Pilates lesson during the Covid era. Prices were not cheap—from 800 RMB/hour to 250 RMB for group classes.

Despite the high prices, it was actually hard for me to book one-on-one sessions with a trainer. Classes were booked out, mostly with young females in their twenties and thirties. My coach Mira told me I had to book appointments a month in advance for private classes, several days in advance for group classes. The owner of the Pilates chain told me: "My biggest barrier to growth is getting enough good coaches. Getting clients these days is not the major problem, as so many young women are willing to pay to get healthy and in shape."

One twenty-something-year-old woman at the Pilates center who makes 20,000 RMB a month told me she spends 2000–3000 RMB a month on Lululemon clothes because they are "more comfortable" than competitors' and because she likes how she feels about herself when she wears Lululemon, despite the high price. She told me she would spend on travel to see and experience the world and on exercise, but not on luxury goods. Being healthy while traveling is the way to show off for young people.

Looking young

"Welcome to my spa," Fatty Wang said, grinning at me as he led me to his spa—it was relatively small with six treatment rooms but high-end with well-trained skin specialists. The average ticket price was 100 USD for a facial popular among Chinese young people.

Aside from spending on physical activities, young women are also spending more money on skincare trying to maintain a youthful appearance. Chinese youth spend more than foreign counterparts on skincare as a percentage of income but less on colored makeup. While they are starting to spend more on lipstick and eyeshadows, they focus on protecting their skin, which is why you will see young Chinese women using umbrellas on sunny days to shield themselves from the sun or paying for Thermage® like Isabelle "the Princess."

Youth are willing to spend on beauty and increasingly want domestic brands like Fan Bingbing's facial care line because they are made by Chinese for Chinese. Chinese will still buy foreign brands like L'Oréal but the days of easy wins for foreign brands are gone. Chinese no longer view foreign cosmetic brands as necessarily better than domestic brands.

Domestic players are moving up the value chain and seen as catering better to the needs of Chinese skin types. Foreign brands still have opportunities in China but they need to make sure their recipes and marketing are geared specifically for the Chinese consumer or else they will be outcompeted by local brands.

Most marketers who have not visited China since Covid are surprised at how different Chinese young people are from their pre-Covid counterparts, affecting how marketing campaigns resonate and how marketing budgets are allocated. Young people are no longer brimming with optimism, ready to become masters of the universe and take over the world. They are now anxious and stressed and cautious in how they spend their money. They want to buy brands where they can display their uniqueness. Brands need to carve out niches and emphasize their brand heritage in order to differentiate their goods from the cheap but good-quality ones coming straight from the factory.

Instead of spending on physical items to show off, young people now focus on spending on experiences like travel or exercise classes. When they do buy physical items, it is often on products like yoga pants or hiking boots that are used in conjunction with experiences centered on being healthy.

This change in spending patterns is not a short-term shift due to a weak economy post-Covid but an ingrained, long-term pivot. Much like those raised in the Great Depression in America, young people who grew up during Covid will forever be more cautious in their spending patterns than youth in the pre-Covid era. They will save more for rainy days and spend more on spirituality, health, and wellness.

Notes

1. Jacob Funk Kirkegaard, "China's Population Decline is Getting Close to Irreversible," *PIIE*, January 18, 2024, https://www.piie.com/research/piie-charts/2024/chinas-population-decline-getting-close-irreversible
2. Staff Writers, "Marriage Age Increases as Ratio of Couples Aged 25–39 Rises," *Global Times*, October 15, 2023, https://www.globaltimes.cn/page/202310/1299902.shtml
3. Vanessa Cai, "Study Reveals Mental Health Impact of Shanghai's Harsh Covid Lockdown," *South China Morning Post*, March 26, 2023, https://www.scmp.com/news/china/politics/article/3214767/study-reveals-mental-health-impact-shanghais-harsh-Covid-lockdown

CHAPTER 15

An Aging Population

Originally from Shanghai, the 58-year-old Mr. Wang typifies the rich in China who gained wealth from China's real estate boom of 2003–8. During those five golden years, risk-taking investors could buy homes with few limits on the number of housing units an individual could buy. Without no minimum down payments required, speculators like Mr. Wang became uber wealthy by buying dozens or even hundreds of residential units. They would flip homes to pay off debts and buy more homes. Flipping homes is what Mr. Wang did to become rich, buying scores of residential apartments before selling them months later after prices soared.

By the start of the Beijing Olympics in 2008, worries over a real estate bubble emerged, so the government tried to put the brakes on the frenzy—prices had become too high in Tier 1 cities like Shanghai and Beijing, exacerbating income disparity between regions. Even in those years, the government worried developers built too much without real underlying demand that could cause a real estate crisis that threatened the financial system. Nothing the government did though stopped construction and rising prices—banks, real estate developers and consumers all wanted the party to continue as they got rich from soaring real estate prices. To reduce risk the government implemented limits on the number of housing units one could buy and hiked up down payments.

Even with the new restrictions, Chinese just kept buying and buying real estate. Real estate investing was viewed as a sure thing. Mr. Wang also profited during the lesser but still extensive real estate boom from 2008 to 2018. Home buyers had to put 30 percent down for an apartment in a high rise and 50 percent and sometimes even 100 percent down for a villa with a garden (depending upon the city and district). In most cities, only people with a local *hukou*, or household registration, could buy homes in that city in order to prevent speculators from other areas driving prices up too high for local residents. Housing prices still rose at a 10–20 percent clip annually in most Tier 1 and Tier 2 cities during the second real estate boom. Returns remained high as state-owned banks opened the taps for mortgages, and the equity markets, where fraud was rife, underperformed the real estate sector. Afraid of the equity markets, Chinese preferred to invest in tangible homes in case the economy went south. At least they would have a home to live in or rent out.

During the Golden period, Mr. Wang amassed so many homes he was able to sell properties in the center of Shanghai and keep buying in the outskirts and in other cities where there were fewer buying restrictions but where prices kept soaring. Mr. Wang profited by flipping houses. He did not even bother to renovate the homes—he bought them unfinished as empty concrete shells without wiring that looked like parking garages and sold them unfinished. Prices rose so quickly that as soon as one was allowed to buy a house, one did so—out of fear that prices would continue to rise.

Mr. Wang used the names of his kids and grandkids to flip homes throughout China, raking in millions in profit annually. He never kept properties to rent out, but just flipped them and then used the capital to buy in cheaper districts or cities. Rental yields were low, about a quarter of yields in the US, as few Chinese wanted to rent, so Mr. Wang just bought and sold homes.

"I bought one villa for 2 million USD in 2011 right in the heart of Jinqiao," Mr. Wang told me to illustrate how he made money. Set up originally to cater to expats with generous housing allowances who wanted to live in standalone villas and send their kids to international schools like the Shanghai American School, Jinqiao emerged as hotspot living area for wealthy Chinese. "Five years later I sold my villa in Jinqiao for 5 million USD, making 3 million USD in profit," Mr. Wang told me. He then used 1 million USD of profit to buy another villa on the outskirts of Shanghai, over an hour away from Lujiazui, Shanghai's financial center. He smiled. "Five years later, that home is now worth 4 million USD because a highway opened up, reducing the commute time to Lujiazui to only 20 minutes."

"I took another 2 million USD in profits to invest in California where I developed a small shopping complex there." As he explained further, "More and more Chinese were going to the US didn't have enough good Chinese restaurants where they can get authentic Chinese food so that is why I opened up my shopping and dining plaza."

His plans in California had worked out even better than he expected. The value of his strip mall had doubled in value to 4 million USD, Mr. Wang said, as America enjoyed a real estate boom during Covid when home prices with large backyards soared. He also signed a deal to rent out his shopping plaza for ten years to a middleman investor, guaranteeing him a decade of steady cash flow to use on other investments and to pay for a 1.7 million USD home in California that he said was "double the size of his main home in Shanghai."

By continually flipping his real estate investments, he made 1–3 million USD per flip. He did this multiple times a year, raking in 5–10 million USD annually in profits, he reckoned.

To ensure the wealth of his family, Mr. Wang sent his son and his daughter-in-law to oversee the shopping plaza. In reality, they do not have to do much as the middleman is in charge of overseeing tenants, so they spend most of their time entertaining wealthy Chinese businesspeople so the Wangs gain access to more and more investment deals around the world.

Much like Pierre and Isabelle's husband whom we met in Chapter 12, Mr. Wang's kids are part of the *fuerdai* class that often seem more intent on having fun and spending money than on hard work. They have a steady stream of income and few responsibilities. They have bought Porsches and travel around the world on vacation. However, unlike Pierre, they are good businesspeople in their own right and do not just party with their father's earnings—they buy properties for investment in Japan, Singapore, and Hong Kong and buy and sell stocks in America.

A risk-taking generation

Perhaps surprisingly to many, the biggest risk takers in China's business world are not Chinese youth who, as we saw in the previous chapter, have become cautious and anxious, but Silver Hairs in their mid-fifties and early sixties like Mr. Wang. Many Western businesspeople hold the mistaken belief that older Chinese are conservative and averse to risks because of traditional Chinese cultural stereotypes. That stereotype might be true for Chinese born before 1962—they lost so much during the social and political upheavals of the Great Leap Forward and the Cultural Revolution that they just want steady and stable jobs that pay for health insurance and offer a pension plan.

But, in reality, the age cohort born between 1962 and 1980 has led China's business growth over the last 40 years by taking risks and transforming entire industries. Alibaba's Jack Ma and Tencent's Pony Ma are both in this age group and led China's private sector growth by investing in real estate and business model innovation.

In many ways, Mr. Wang's cohort had no choice but become risk takers if they wanted to become rich—they had to take risks in order to put food on the table. They were in their twenties and early thirties when Prime Minister Zhu Rongji reformed the state-owned sector causing millions to lose their jobs in the mid- to late 1990s. They found that starting private businesses and investing in real estate were more stable than working for SOEs and also potentially more profitable.

They grew up dirt poor and had to scratch and claw their way to wealth. They were young enough to miss the brunt of the Cultural Revolution, so did not experience the stress and depression from having built up something only to have it taken away like older generations. People like Mr. Wang had nothing but the shirts on their backs, so they had to take risks to get ahead by starting companies and investing in real estate. They often took out 100 percent interest rate loans from the informal underground banking economy in the 1990s to launch new ventures. One real estate developer, Mr. Wu, told me that he started his real estate business in Wuhan in the late 1980s by borrowing money to build a skyscraper at a 100 percent interest rate over three months. That's not an annualized 100 percent but over three months! High interest rates are why so many shoddy buildings were built in the 1980s and 1990s: private developers owed so much debt, they cut corners to finish buildings as soon as possible to pay off loans. Mr. Wu estimates he is now worth 600 million USD.

Mr. Wang and Mr. Wu's generation had to the gumption to go all the way: borrowing from loan sharks to get ahead and travelling to places in far-off countries to develop shopping plazas and the like. Mr. Wang does not speak a word of English to this day, but he sent his son overseas to study for college to prepare him for an interconnected global world. His three grandchildren go to international school in Shanghai and are as comfortable in an English-speaking environment as they are in a Chinese one. Their parents plan to send the children to the US or maybe the UK for university.

People like Mr. Wang, and there are millions with similar stories, have benefited from China's rise. While this cohort has generally been supportive of the CPC, its members are starting to look to move more assets offshore and to emigrate to other countries as a fallback plan as they become increasingly worried by Xi's Common Prosperity Drive and how it will impact their family's ability to make money. Their underlying reasons for shifting assets offshore are very different from those of businesspeople who emigrated in the early 2010s, who were often corrupt and concerned they would be arrested under Xi's crackdown or because they opposed Party control. Mr. Wang's generation are shifting assets abroad because they see fewer easy opportunities to make big profits in China. While they generally support the CPC, they are uneasy about the shift toward socialism and the renewed importance of state-owned enterprises in the economy. Never-ending corruption crackdowns have also made them wary that they too might get caught up in the dragnets. As one billionaire told me, "It does not seem like the Party wants really rich people anymore. I need to get money offshore as a backup plan just in case."

For Mr. Wang's age group, the golden days of profiting in the real estate sector and other one-time lucrative deals are over, as Xi's Common Prosperity drive continues. They also see the state sector reemerging to gain control of a wider swathe of sectors, as Xi wants more direct control of over all the levers of the economy for purposes of power and worries over national security threats.

To diversify risk, Silver Hairs like Mr. Wang are buying second, third and fourth homes offshore and looking to move more money offshore. This is why capital flight has become such a problem. One wealthy Shanghainese in his fifties told me, "I bought a villa in Phuket, a house in London, and several properties in the US. I am comfortable traveling and living around the world." Another wealthy Chinese of this generation, a senior executive of a publicly traded Chinese company, told me he had bought a 6 million USD home in New York City because he wanted to get money out just in case.

Some Silver Hairs are semi-retiring like the real estate developer Mr. Wu because they have made enough and do not want to go through the hassle of dealing with Xi's Common Prosperity Drive and the never-ending corruption crackdown. They are often patriotic and would never leave China. They are often just waiting to see where the domestic political winds will blow and decide whether they will get back into the game or retire once and for all. They are also often subsidizing the lives of their children and grandchildren who are not willing to work hard, as we saw in Chapter 14. Covid has made this group reprioritize their lives, too—they want their kids and grandkids to be healthy and happy and less driven to make money.

Still other Silver Hairs like Mr. Wang do not want to retire completely so have set up businesses and buy and sell homes in America, Australia, and other countries that cater to the wave of Chinese immigrants.

To expand abroad, the silver generation often relies on their children and grandchildren. Their kids and grandkids like Mr. Wang's are globally sophisticated and able to conduct business easily in multiple languages and regions—they are as comfortable operating in Sydney, London, and New York as they are in Beijing or Guangzhou. As one billionaire entrepreneur in his early sixties told me, "I gave my son 15 million USD to invest in real estate in the US to diversify our holdings internationally while I still focus on running the business in China. I expect slower growth in China, faster overseas. I will have my son run our overseas investments because he speaks English while I do not."

In other words, wealthy Silver Hairs are keeping one foot in China but putting one foot outside via their children and grandchildren. This is one major reason why SME fixed-asset investment in China has been so low in the post-Covid era. Worried about geopolitics and domestic policies that favor SOEs and the 90 percent, SME business owners have simply stopped investing in China.

When Chinese are unhappy with the economy or political system, they do not protest or push for regime change—they vote with their wallets by moving money offshore. For their holdings within China, they reallocate RMB holdings away from real estate and equities and into fixed-term deposits and life insurance policies. They just want to maintain their wealth rather than lose it.

Silver Hair shopping trends

Even though they might be nervous to draw the attention of tax authorities by spending on big-ticket, flashy items like new homes and Ferraris in China, Mr. Wang and his generational cohort remain a great market to sell to both within and especially outside China as they set up businesses focused on China and businesses focused on the rest of the world. They also have homes in multiple countries. For many of them, they still buy lifestyle goods—cars, homes, and luxury items—to show that they have attained a certain level of success and status in life both in China and abroad where they have their second and third homes and where Chinese tax authorities don't have jurisdiction.

Not only does Mr. Wang epitomize his age group of daring risk takers, but he also indicates a new trend emerging—generational wealth transference. As we saw in Chapter 12 on *fuerdai*, the great wealth generated by this generation is starting to be transferred to their children and grandchildren. Their offspring are globally sophisticated in luxury trends and brands. They most likely have spent their youth in Western nations studying. Their incomes are secure because they receive allowances from their parents. The weak real estate sector in the post-Covid world is unsettling for them so they are cutting back on some big-ticket items, but they still power 50 percent of the consumer economy.

Mr. Wang told me that preserving wealth and giving opportunities to later generations is why he went all the way to California. He is in the process of transferring his holdings to his children to give them a platform to earn money on their own while also trying to avoid possible inheritance taxes. Transference of wealth provides a great opportunity for the professional services industry, especially for wealth management companies.

The real estate developer Mr. Wu told me: "I have had made so much money in real estate during the go-go days that it would be virtually impossible for my daughter to make as much as I did unless she got lucky as an entrepreneur and took a company IPO." Mr. Wu sent his daughter to an Ivy League school. She is working killer hours in a bulge-bracket investment bank to get training. Eventually, Mr. Wu wants his daughter to run his real estate empire and use her training to preserve the wealth he created rather than earn her own riches through banking.

Many Chinese have gotten so rich that, like Mr. Wu, they worry their children will lose the family nest egg if they are not trained properly—they do not necessarily care whether the younger generations are able to increase the family wealth, more that they able to preserve it. Steady and stable asset growth is their goal at this stage, much like it was for wealthy Americans like the Rockefellers and Vanderbilts who put wealth into multigenerational trusts and tax-free municipal bonds to preserve wealth long-term.

A lost generation

While Mr. Wang and Mr. Wu and their generation profited from China's post 1978 reforms and the embrace of capitalism, those born in the 1940s and 1950s who are now in their seventies and eighties, on the other hand, are a lost generation of sorts. This older generation have faced tremendous upheaval and uncertainty during their lives—from World War II through the Civil War and Cultural Revolution to the Covid era. They were too old to benefit from the economic reforms starting in 1978. For them, maintaining a steady, stable job at a SOE was the pinnacle of success so they could always put food on the table. They often also missed out on Xi's sweeping reforms that gave people health insurance because they have always saved for a rainy day. By nature and experience, they are far more conservative than Mr. Wang's Silver Hair generation. They are, in many ways, similar to the Chinese youth of today who, anxious about the future, are also saving hard. One major difference between the two groups is that the older generation never made much money so were desperate and willing to toil long hours unlike the young people of today, their grandchildren, who "lie flat."

When brands look at targeting the older generations in China, they should not target those born in the 1940s and 1950s as the decision-makers but their children who make purchasing decisions for them. Aside from being conservative spenders, elderly Chinese never learned how to use apps and other mobile services until the Covid era when they were forced to do so in order to get Covid tests.

This older generation suffered during Covid because they had never used apps to purchase groceries and were thus unable to buy food during lockdowns. Many spent three years hiding in their homes because the need to use a mobile phone to scan health codes to enter buildings was too difficult and stressful. As one 82-year-old women in Beijing, Mrs. Wang, told me, "I did not eat in an indoor restaurant during the entire Covid period because I was too scared. I even asked my kids and grandkids to limit visits to me." Even though zero-Covid is over, she rarely goes outside her home into malls and restaurants—she spends most of her time with her family in outdoor areas like parks because she remains afraid of catching Covid.

Like many older Chinese, Mrs. Wang spent much less during the Covid era because figuring out how to use mobile apps was too difficult or they relied on their kids or grandkids to make purchase decisions for them. Her kids bought her products on ecommerce sites and had food and other items delivered to her.

The government is very protective of this generation and explains why it took so long for the government to end zero-Covid and why there was never a countrywide vaccine requirement—they worried the older generation would succumb to Covid and did not push vaccinations campaigns for fear of side effects. They are also the most likely to be swindled in the fraud scams that run rampant in China today. Telecom scams especially, often run by Chinese gangs operating overseas in Cambodia or the Philippines, target the elderly with "get rich quick" investment scams.

The government is trying to crack down on scams that target older Chinese and end telecom fraud. There have been mass arrests of gangs engaged in the scams. Trying to stop telecom fraud is why some provinces have banned incoming texts and calls from overseas unless the phone owner directly signs up to receive international calls. The Western media has portrayed such bans as examples of Xi's demand for control and wish to cut China off from the rest of the world, though the truth is that the government is trying to stop gangs targeting the elderly.

My immediate family was the target of an attempted telecom scam where a fraudster called up my wife. He had all of our details including ID information for the entire extended family. He said he was a policeman and that we had to transfer money immediately to pay a fine because we were under investigation for fraud and insider dealing with a bank where we had a savings account. He knew which bank we had money with and some of our confidential account information. His story sounded plausible.

The fake police officer claimed that it was our financial advisor who had stolen money and that we might be implicated, which is why we needed to pay a fine. He said that, if we were ultimately found not guilty, then the money would be returned to us—the fine was to ensure that we would not try to flee the country. Luckily for us, we did not fall for the scam and called the public security bureau for advice. The officer looked into the matter and said it was clearly a fraud, though a very sophisticated one.

Selling to Silver Hairs

When brands look at the best ways to expand in China, it is all about building trust when selling to the Silver Hairs and the elderly populations. Brands need to understand that, because of rampant fraud, older people and their children spend a long time researching products and services because they are scared of being cheated and falling victim to crime. Decision-making becomes a family discussion. Marketing campaigns have to reflect this family and intergenerational decision-making process. They also tend to trust big, large brands with long histories more than newer brands, even those offering great-quality products. They just buy what they know and tried-and-tested brands.

American baby boomers buy homes and stocks with little input from their children and remain financially independent as long as possible, but that is largely not the case in China. Older generations rely on their children to help ensure they do not get scammed.

Mr. Wang's generation and their offspring also provide opportunities for businesses in other countries as they shift assets out of China. They buy real estate, gold, and homes overseas for their children and send their kids abroad for schooling and medical care. Brands needs to build a reputation for trust if they are going to sell to China's Silver Hairs and elderly. Chinese in their fifties and sixties remain battle-hardened, risk-taking businesspeople. They are a prime group to sell to—they have overcome and succeeded during difficult times and spend to enjoy their lives and ensure a long-term quality of life for their children and grandchildren. While they might not be cosmopolitan or well educated themselves, they are sophisticated and forward thinking—after all, they prepared their children for an international lifestyle. Unlike Chinese just a few years older who are conservative, they tend be the main decision-makers—risk-taking and confident.

CHAPTER 16

Chinese Women's Empowerment

"Should I buy a BMW X5 or a Porsche 911?" 41-year-old Tiffany asked me while we were having Peking duck for lunch in Beijing. Originally from Fujian, Tiffany is the managing partner of the Beijing operations for an American consulting firm. Under her direction, the firm's sales beat expectations by 75 percent over the previous three years. Recognizing Tiffany's business development abilities, the global partners offered her to become one of the youngest ever equity partners when she was 38.

Tiffany's rise to the top of her firm is typical of many female executives in the private sector in China and indicates a breakdown in traditional gender roles. After she joined the firm on graduation from a top Chinese university, Tiffany quickly rose up the ranks. She now out-earns her husband, five years her senior, who works at a different consulting firm.

Eager to enjoy the fruits of her labor, she was thinking about buying a BMW, a Li Xiang, or a Porsche—she, not her husband, was the main decision-maker for their family of three's auto purchases.

Tiffany represents a shift happening at the more senior levels of companies—a trend that foreign brands need to understand: even in sectors like the automotive industry where sales and decision-making have been traditionally driven by men, women are now becoming the main decision-makers—whether to buy a cheaper brand like BYD or an expensive one like Mercedes or Porsche. They are used to making decisions in the office and are making more of the decisions at home.

Moreover, as China shifts to a service economy based on brains rather than an export or infrastructure economy driven by raw physical might, more women are becoming the main breadwinners of their families. Women are out-earning men even within poorer families living in rural areas where traditional family structures and gender norms are more likely to be in place.

Salaries in the service sector toward which women gravitate, like restaurants or retail, are higher than those in manufacturing or construction where men still dominate because of the need for raw strength. As one 32-year-old waitress from Anhui Province told me, "I am working in Shanghai where I can get a high salary in a restaurant, while my husband has stayed in our hometown working in construction. I earn double what he does, which I'm proud of, but he can now spend more time with our son, which I am jealous of."

The biggest big-ticket items Chinese buy are houses, cars, and education for children. Traditionally, men dominated the decision-making process for these sectors, but we now see that successful career women like Tiffany are now the major decision-makers. She is also the main decision-maker on where to send her daughter to school—she wants to send her to the US or the UK for boarding school and then university. Brands need to take account of this shift in decision-making power and change their marketing campaigns accordingly.

Too many brands import advertising campaigns that worked overseas in America or Europe without much thought of how campaigns will be received by Chinese females. Slogans often don't translate easily. Companies need to create marketing campaigns that fit Chinese female consumer tastes and aspirations.

Women earning high salaries in the private sector are leading the consumer revolution in China's post-Covid world and driving sales—whether that's dining out, luxury jewelry, or outdoor apparel. Too many brands do not realize the shift in consumption decision-making taking place and continue to target the traditional—but wrong—target market—middle-aged males. Aside from having the purchasing power to shop directly for themselves, Chinese women in their fifties and below are starting to heavily influence decision-making in sectors like cars that were once the purview of Chinese men. Silver Hair-generation women are also deciding what to buy, as we saw in Chapter 15. Brands that still favor men in advertising campaigns as a default are making a grave mistake as women are increasingly influential in making purchasing decisions, even in sectors once dominated by male shoppers. Mercedes, for example, has thrived by targeting females in its marketing campaigns—not just female senior executives driven around by their chauffeurs but also women who drive themselves around. Mercedes' smaller cars like the A and B classes are popular among women wanting a prestigious brand that's also cute. As one 40-year-old woman in Shanghai, who drives a Mercedes B-class, told me, "I wanted to have a luxury car to make myself happy." China is Mercedes largest market in the world for a reason—it targets not just traditional segments like males and business executives but also female executives and millennials.

Eventually, Tiffany decided to buy a Porsche Cayenne Turbo—she liked the sporty nature of the 911 but ultimately decided she wanted a bigger car so that she feels safe driving in traffic and for her daughter's soccer and other sports equipment. Tiffany told me driving such a sporty but large SUV made her feel powerful. In her case, she said, she chose the Turbo version of the Cayenne because she like the color of the paint rather than because of the extra power. This was the main reason she chose the more expensive Porsche—cheaper versions did not have the mix of colors she wanted. Different consumers will have different purchasing motivations. In cars, for example, to varying degrees speed, handling, horsepower, color choices, seat comfort, and passenger and storage spaces will all rank differently in consumer's priorities. Understanding what combination of factors motivates women, rather than men, to buy products will be critical for brands in product development and marketing.

Delaying marriage and childbirth

I had just finished eating a giant pot of spicy Sichuanese hotpot when I met Kathy, a 32-year-old Sichuanese woman. She had an ambitious air about her. She wore a dark-black pantsuit and her dyed brown hair was tied back in a bun.

With my mouth still tingling from the *mala* spice of the hotpot, I asked her what she did for a living. She told me that she was working in the hotel business in a big international hospitality chain: "I hope one day to be promoted to general manager. I would prefer to stay in an international chain like Hyatt because the corporate culture is better than in a Chinese hotel chain." She continued: "The hours are tough in hospitality but I'm driven to succeed. The long hours are one of the reasons that makes it difficult for me to find a husband and to have children. But right now, my goal is to succeed in my career. I want to succeed in business first, then I can think about maybe having a family once I reach my career goals."

Kathy epitomizes career and family trends in today's China for women in the private sector—they are marrying later, if at all, because they want to focus on their careers before settling down. Marrying late as Kathy plans to do is also one of the key reasons for China's low birth rate and aging population, as we saw previously.

Historically, young women from peasant families like Kathy would marry in their early twenties. Often, they did not know much about birth control and would get pregnant as soon as they started having sex with their first boyfriend. Out of a mix of duty and shame, they would marry their boyfriend, even though they did not truly love him. As one 31-year-old from Jiangsu told me, "We had sex when I was a teenager, and I got pregnant right away. We married, even though I did not really know him. What a mistake."

The official minimum marrying age is 20 for women, 22 for men. The CPC actually set the minimum age relatively high because too many teenage girls had been pushed into early marriages by their families under both Imperial and Nationalist rule. Still, many women continue to marry early because they have had babies due to limited access to or knowledge about contraceptives—marriages cobbled together because of accidental pregnancies explain the soaring divorce rate in China among couples under the age of 40—almost 50 percent.

For Kathy, her ambition in life was not just about getting married and having a kid. Her family supported her in her career ambitions, she said, and did not pressure her to marry too soon. Perhaps counterintuitively, the one-child policy has helped women like Kathy move to the top of the corporate ladder in the private sector. Instead of placing their hopes and dreams on male heirs, families placed their hopes on their children regardless of gender. Daughters became as important as sons and were pushed to be ambitious. As Layla, a

27-year-old Shanghainese woman who graduated from Columbia University with a Master's degree told me, "I never want to get married. Even if I do, I do not want to have children because that will stop me in my career aspirations. My parents support me in my career goals."

"Leftover Women"

Bucking traditional gender norms, many women like Layla are deciding not to get married at all. These are often well-educated women who have studied abroad and earn high salaries. Often called Leftover Women, these women who choose not to get married demonstrate that gender equality is improving in China. Some Western analysts say Leftover Women is a degrading term, but the trend is actually the result of female empowerment. Women are not being forced into marriages or made to feel that having a baby determines and defines their worth. Women build successful careers on their own like Tiffany and are not being pressured to marry for the sake of marrying and conforming to cultural norms of the family unit like Kathy and Layla. Many women simply have not found a man whom they consider to be a good fit and do not feel pressured to marry for the sake of getting married, which would have happened to previous generations.

One 40-year-old single woman from Shandong Province told me, "My parents have not pressured me to get married. They have seen how successful and happy I am with my career. I am sure they want me to get married but they want me to find the right person. I do hope I will get married one day, but I need to find the right person. If it is not meant to be, then it is not meant to be. I am happy to stay single forever. I won't settle."

Her words mirror those told me by Janice, a 36-year-old woman from Beijing, who works in investment banking. Her father was previously a minister in a key ministry. He had not pressured her to get married despite many suitors. Janice said, "He just wants me to be happy. I am happy being single."

Glass ceilings in officialdom

The shift toward female empowerment in China started under Mao Zedong when he famously said, "Women hold up half of the sky," and pushed for women to have more equality in Chinese society. Under Mao, the CPC combatted traditional Confucian gender norms where women were subservient to men. Mao abolished foot-binding and concubinage and eradicated prostitution. The government also launched mass campaigns for women to have equal education opportunities and empowered wives with the right to initiate divorce.

Gender equality has paid dividends for Chinese society from economic and human rights standpoints. In 1990, 87 percent of males were literate while only 68 percent of females were. For those born after 1990, there is near literacy parity by gender—99.8 percent for men, 99.6 percent for women.

By the 2010s, more Chinese women pursued a university education than men. Overall, 50.6 percent of women choose to pursue higher education, and they compromise 51.7 percent of students in China's undergraduate student population.[1] It is true that at Tsinghua University, Xi Jinping's alma mater (often referred to as the MIT of China), there are still more men to women with a ratio of 33:17, though this is considerably up from 5:1 just two decades before.[2] Clearly, Tsinghua is on the right path but still needs to do a better job at attracting and welcoming female students.

Despite the ratio at Tsinghua, the trend lines are clear for China in higher education—women are increasingly getting educational opportunities equal to those open to men and this is having a direct benefit on the quality of their lives and on society overall. Chinese women like Tiffany and Kathy have become the major growth driver for consumer product companies like Canada Goose, Apple, and Costa Coffee as they have scored good jobs in the private sector.

However, most female empowerment has been concentrated in women working in the private sector, like Tiffany and Kathy. Despite's Mao's push for gender equality in society, women have yet to reach gender parity in officialdom or in state-owned enterprises (SOEs) where senior officials remain predominantly men. Since the early 2000s, the CPC did not appoint a woman to be a member of the Politburo at the 20th People's Congress. Typically, a woman secured at least one spot at the higher echelons of power in China, often a vice premier position. Vice Premier Wu Yi during the Hu Jintao administration led China's economic discussions with the US with her counterpart, Hank Paulson, treasury secretary and former CEO of Goldman Sachs. Under Xi's second term as president, Vice Premier Sun Chunlan was charged with containing Covid and is widely seen as responsible for ending the draconian policies during the Shanghai lockdown. Both Wu and Sun are regarded highly by the Chinese people as capable and caring for the people.

No woman, however, was appointed to a senior position for Xi's third term. The lack of women and gender parity in previous administrations in the 1980s, 1990s, and even early 2000s is arguably understandable—few women were educated before the communist era and thus might not have qualified or entered the Party's ranks in the 1950s to 1970s, preferring to go into the budding private sector, take a stable but low-profile job to avoid political troubles, or stay at home.

The omission for women is inexcusable now in the latest Congress as many women are qualified—they are well educated and have paid their political dues during the last 40 years of the reform era. Enough talented and well-trained women are senior enough to deserve powerful roles not just with a vice premier position but also within the seven-member standing committee of the Politburo, China's highest decision-making organ. Criticisms of the lack of female representation within the most senior government positions during Xi's third term are well justified.

Moreover, the state-owned sector also is not welcoming enough to women aspiring to senior positions in the hierarchy. Men dominate proceedings. Often, women are left to take notes or pour alcohol and tea for guests. SOEs also often put up barriers to women getting promoted if they also want to have children. One female executive told me many subsidiaries of SOEs will not appoint a woman as a general manager unless they agree verbally not to have a child for five years. She herself was deciding whether to have a child or to apply for promotion to a general manager position. This is a dilemma no woman should have to face—pursue a career or have a family. Such stipulations are illegal under Chinese employment law, but the government does not enforce the law often enough, allowing unwritten company rules to continue. This is also a reason why there is an aging population in China, with women choosing to pursue their careers and delay having a family.

The lack of female representation in SOEs is one reason state actors are often slow to innovate and keep abreast of market trends when compared with private enterprises that encourage female participation.

The way to promotion often involves boys' nights out drinking distilled Chinese liquor like *maotai* or *wuliangye* until cadres are on the verge of passing out. I have seen ambitious female executives try to keep up with drinking games, but often they cannot, or they are viewed as not being part of the team because they don't join in enough. Despite campaigns against drinking on the job by Xi, banquets where officials down bottles of alcohol are frequent. As SOEs regain more influence in Xi's China, it will be critical for them to attract more high-end female talent if they want to remain as efficient and innovative as the private sector. Until they do that, SOEs will often be laggards at adopting new trends.

While the political arena too often boxes women out of senior roles, and there remain barriers at the senior levels of SOEs, the private sector benefits from well-educated, ambitious women who are taking charge of companies and leading private sector growth. Half of the world's female billionaires are Chinese, and many females are at the top of private companies, like Meng Wanzhou, the heir apparent at Huawei. Joey Wat is the CEO of YUM China and has led the growth of KFC and Pizza Hut, and Jane Sun is the CEO of Trip.com, China's largest travel operator. As one CEO of China for a financial services Fortune 500 multinational corporation told me, "We have more women than men in our white-collar positions—they tend to be more easily trained and more loyal than many males."

Over the next decade, retail sales and growth will continue to be powered by Chinese women under the age of 50 who work in the private sector. As China continues to be an economy based on brains rather than brawn, better-educated women will continue to climb the private sector corporate ladder. Because they are often unable to rise through the ranks of officialdom, this gives private sector companies the opportunity to hire the best talent out of half the population.

Many of these Chinese women are marrying later and have emerged as equal decision-makers to men once they get married. They are not willing to play traditional, subservient gender roles. Marriages are becoming partnerships of equals.

Brands need to rethink who they target in marketing campaigns. For many companies, targeting middle-aged men will no longer drive growth—targeting women in their forties like Tiffany or young females in their twenties and thirties like Layla and Kathy will likely drive growth.

What women want can often differ from what men want. To inform product development and marketing campaigns, companies need to understand the underlying reasons why females buy products. Take Tiffany, for example, who cared more about having a wide range of color choices for paintwork on her car than she had a focus on its engine and speed. Going forward, brands need to understand what motivates Chinese women to purchase a product or service more than ever before—such an understanding will help drive growth and shape decisions for more and more brands in the future.

Notes

1. Staff Writers, "More Than Half of China's Junior College, University Students are Female: White Paper," *Xinhua News*, August 12, 2021, http://www.news.cn/english/2021-08/12/c_1310122992.htm
2. Olivia Halsall, "Chinese Women in Elite Spaces," *Diplomat*, April 13, 2020, https://thediplomat.com/2020/04/chinese-women-in-elite-spaces/

Epilogue

In the post-Covid era, I have traveled around the world—from America to Saudi Arabia to Australia—to give keynotes and meet with investors and businesspeople about the opportunities China holds. I have spoken with hundreds of hedge fund managers and senior executives about how China has changed because of Covid and geopolitical tension and what China's government is doing to deal with a broken growth playbook.

During my discussions, I found that, because China's borders were virtually closed for three full years, and because many Western journalists have not been in China during that time or do not speak Chinese, misinformation, disinformation, and unfounded fears about China's trajectory dominated the conversation. Many investors and businesspeople did not understand the direction the Chinese government was taking the country in or the underlying reasons for crackdowns and other initiatives. Anxious and uninformed, too many businesspeople thought China was un-investable. Many told me they were scared to visit China because they thought they would be arrested simply for being foreign.

Yet, despite the very real risks facing China's economy outlined in this book, no country holds the potential China has to power a third of global growth over the next five years. Fears that China has become antibusiness are also exaggerated. China cracked down and reformed the education, health care, and education sectors in order to help grow the size of the middle class and unlock their spending power. Fears over the crackdowns and so-called arbitrary detentions and arrests of Western executives are exaggerated by US media looking for eyeballs and sensationalist stories. Unless you are breaking the law or are a spy, China remains super safe for foreign executives, perhaps safer than any country in the world.

Recognizing the need for foreign direct investment to help shift the economy toward new growth drivers like NEVs to replace aging ones like real estate, the Chinese government is rolling out the red carpet for foreign businesses more than I have seen in decades. With all the new subsidies, tax breaks, and eased visa policies, China is arguably more open to foreign investment now than at any time in its history.

For investors and businesspeople looking to profit, China is the next China. Let me repeat that—China is the next China. Unless you are in a sector like semiconductors that the US—not China—prevents from expanding in the country, China should remain the largest or one of the main growth drivers for most companies and investors. No other country, not even India, has the scale to replace China as a growth driver in the next five years.

When others are scared, be greedy. For those with enough capital to take a medium- to longer-term view and who can navigate the challenging domestic and international political situations, this will be seen as a golden age to invest in China.

Don't get me wrong—China is not the no-brainer, not-to-be-missed place to invest in it used to be. The risks are higher than at any time in my three decades here but so are the rewards. No country, not the US, not Vietnam, not India, has the potential to account for one-third of global growth in the next five years. Now is the time for companies with the stomach for high risk, high returns.

That's me. I am doubling down and hiring and expanding my firm, the China Market Research Group (CMR), that I founded in 2005. The question is: Are you willing to take the risk for what could again be the world's greatest growth engine, or are you going to let fear and disinformation stand in your way?